"After utilizing toolkits from The Art of Service, I was able to identify threats within my organization to which I was completely unaware. Using my team's knowledge as a competitive advantage, we now have superior systems that save time and energy."

"As a new Chief Technology Officer, I was feeling unprepared and inadequate to be successful in my role. I ordered an IT toolkit Sunday night and was prepared Monday morning to shed light on areas of improvement within my organization. I no longer felt overwhelmed and intimidated, I was excited to share what I had learned."

"I used the questionnaires to interview members of my team. I never knew how many insights we could produce collectively with our internal knowledge."

"I usually work until at least 8pm on weeknights. The Art of Service questionnaire saved me so much time and worry that Thursday night I attended my son's soccer game without sacrificing my professional obligations."

"After purchasing The Art of Service toolkit, I was able to identify areas where my company was not in compliance that could have put my job at risk. I looked like a hero when I proactively educated my team on the risks and presented a solid solution."

"I spent months shopping for an external consultant before realizing that The Art of Service would allow my team to consult themselves! Not only did we save time not catching a consultant up to speed, we were able to keep our company information and industry secrets confidential."

"Everyday there are new regulations and processes in my industry. The Art of Service toolkit has kept me ahead by using AI technology to constantly update the toolkits and address emerging needs."

"I customized The Art of Service toolkit to focus specifically on the concerns of my role and industry. I didn't have to waste time with a generic self-help book that wasn't tailored to my exact situation."

"Many of our competitors have asked us about our secret sauce. When I tell them it's the knowledge we have in-house, they never believe me. Little do they know The Art of Service toolkits are working behind the scenes."

"One of my friends hired a consultant who used the knowledge gained working with his company to advise their competitor. Talk about a competitive disadvantage! The Art of Service allowed us to keep our knowledge from walking out the door along with a huge portion of our budget in consulting fees."

"Honestly, I didn't know what I didn't know. Before purchasing The Art of Service, I didn't realize how many areas of my business needed to be refreshed and improved. I am so relieved The Art of Service was there to highlight our blind spots."

"Before The Art of Service, I waited eagerly for consulting company reports to come out each month. These reports kept us up to speed but provided little value because they put our competitors on the same playing field. With The Art of Service, we have uncovered unique insights to drive our business forward."

"Instead of investing extensive resources into an external consultant, we can spend more of our budget towards pursuing our company goals and objectives...while also spending a little more on corporate holiday parties."

"The risk of our competitors getting ahead has been mitigated because The Art of Service has provided us with a 360-degree view of threats within our organization before they even arise."

## Synthetic data
## Complete Self-Assessment Guide

# Table of Contents

# About The Art of Service

The Art of Service, Business Process Architects since 2000, is dedicated to helping stakeholders achieve excellence.

Defining, designing, creating, and implementing a process to solve a stakeholders challenge or meet an objective is the most valuable role… In EVERY group, company, organization and department.

Unless you're talking a one-time, single-use project, there should be a process. Whether that process is managed and implemented by humans, AI, or a combination of the two, it needs to be designed by someone with a complex enough perspective to ask the right questions.

Someone capable of asking the right questions and step back and say, 'What are we really trying to accomplish here? And is there a different way to look at it?'

With The Art of Service's Self-Assessments, we empower people who can do just that — whether their title is marketer, entrepreneur, manager, salesperson, consultant, Business Process Manager, executive assistant, IT Manager, CIO etc... —they are the people who rule the future. They are people who watch the process as it happens, and ask the right questions to make the process work better.

**Contact us when you need any support with this Self-Assessment and any help with templates, blue-prints and examples of standard documents you might need:**

https://theartofservice.com
support@theartofservice.com

# Included Resources - how to access

**Included with your purchase of the book is the Synthetic data**

**Self-Assessment Spreadsheet Dashboard which contains all questions and Self-Assessment areas and auto-generates insights, graphs, and project RACI planning - all with examples to get you started right away.**

How? Simply send an email to
**access@theartofservice.com**
with this books' title in the subject to get the Synthetic data Self Assessment Tool right away.

The auto reply will guide you further, you will then receive the following contents with New and Updated specific criteria:

- The latest quick edition of the book in PDF
- The latest complete edition of the book in PDF, which criteria correspond to the criteria in...
- The Self-Assessment Excel Dashboard, and...
- Example pre-filled Self-Assessment Excel Dashboard to get familiar with results generation
- In-depth specific Checklists covering the topic
- Project management checklists and templates to assist with implementation

**INCLUDES LIFETIME SELF ASSESSMENT UPDATES**

Every self assessment comes with Lifetime Updates and Lifetime Free Updated Books. Lifetime Updates is an industry-first feature which allows you to receive verified self assessment updates, ensuring you always have the most accurate information at your fingertips.

Get it now- you will be glad you did - do it now, before you forget.

Send an email to **access@theartofservice.com** with this books' title in the subject to get the Synthetic data Self Assessment Tool right away.

# Purpose of this Self-Assessment

This Self-Assessment has been developed to improve understanding of the requirements and elements of Synthetic data, based on best practices and standards in business process architecture, design and quality management.

It is designed to allow for a rapid Self-Assessment to determine how closely existing management practices and procedures correspond to the elements of the Self-Assessment.

The criteria of requirements and elements of Synthetic data have been rephrased in the format of a Self-Assessment questionnaire, with a seven-criterion scoring system, as explained in this document.

In this format, even with limited background knowledge of Synthetic data, a manager can quickly review existing operations to determine how they measure up to the standards. This in turn can serve as the starting point of a 'gap analysis' to identify management tools or system elements that might usefully be implemented in the organization to help improve overall performance.

# How to use the Self-Assessment

On the following pages are a series of questions to identify to what extent your Synthetic data initiative is complete in comparison to the requirements set in standards.

To facilitate answering the questions, there is a space in front of each question to enter a score on a scale of '1' to '5'.

1 Strongly Disagree

2 Disagree

3 Neutral

4 Agree

5 Strongly Agree

*Read the question and rate it with the following in front of mind:*

**'In my belief,
the answer to this question is clearly defined'.**

There are two ways in which you can choose to interpret this statement;

1. how aware are you that the answer to the question is clearly defined
2. for more in-depth analysis you can choose to gather evidence and confirm the answer to the question. This obviously will take more time, most Self-Assessment users opt for the first way to interpret the question and dig deeper later on based on the outcome of the overall Self-Assessment.

A score of '1' would mean that the answer is not clear at all, where a '5' would mean the answer is crystal clear and defined. Leave emtpy when the question is not applicable or you don't want to answer it, you can skip it without affecting your score. Write your score in the space provided.

After you have responded to all the appropriate statements in each section, compute your average score for that section, using the formula provided, and round to the nearest tenth. Then transfer to the corresponding spoke in the Synthetic data Scorecard on the second next page of the Self-Assessment.

Your completed Synthetic data Scorecard will give you a clear presentation of which Synthetic data areas need attention.

# Synthetic data Scorecard Example

Example of how the finalized Scorecard can look like:

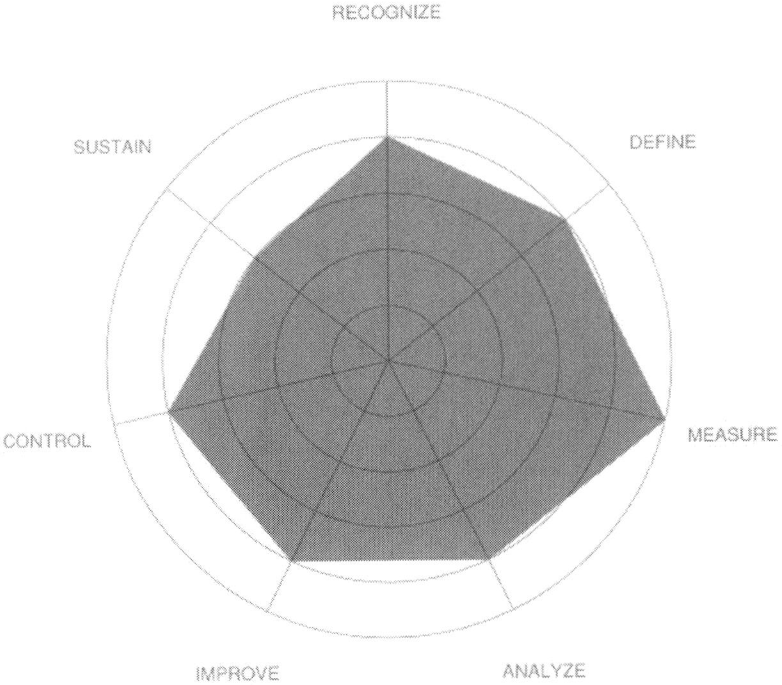

# Synthetic data Scorecard

Your Scores:

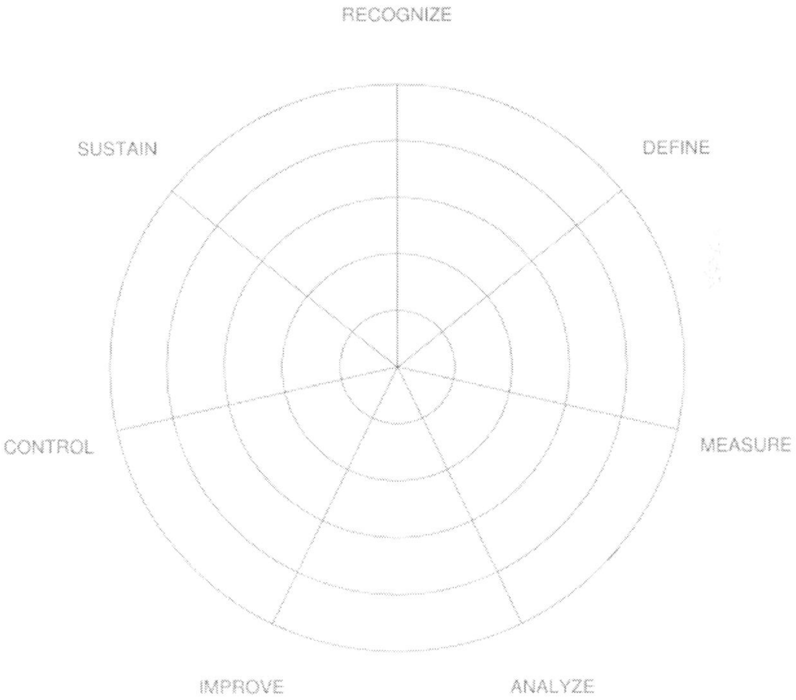

# BEGINNING OF THE SELF-ASSESSMENT:

# CRITERION #1: RECOGNIZE

INTENT: Be aware of the need for change. Recognize that there is an unfavorable variation, problem or symptom.

In my belief, the answer to this question is clearly defined:

5 Strongly Agree

4 Agree

3 Neutral

2 Disagree

1 Strongly Disagree

1. Are there recognized Synthetic data problems?
<--- Score

2. Will Synthetic data deliverables need to be tested and, if so, by whom?
<--- Score

3. Do you need to avoid or amend any Synthetic data activities?

<--- Score

4. To what extent does each concerned units management team recognize Synthetic data as an effective investment?
<--- Score

5. Are problem definition and motivation clearly presented?
<--- Score

6. Who defines the rules in relation to any given issue?
<--- Score

7. Are there any revenue recognition issues?
<--- Score

8. Do you recognize Synthetic data achievements?
<--- Score

9. How do you take a forward-looking perspective in identifying Synthetic data research related to market response and models?
<--- Score

10. To what extent would your organization benefit from being recognized as a award recipient?
<--- Score

11. For your Synthetic data project, identify and describe the business environment, is there more than one layer to the business environment?
<--- Score

12. Are employees recognized or rewarded for performance that demonstrates the highest levels of

integrity?
<--- Score

13. What are the minority interests and what amount of minority interests can be recognized?
<--- Score

14. Identify an operational issue in your organization, for example, could a particular task be done more quickly or more efficiently by Synthetic data?
<--- Score

15. How much are sponsors, customers, partners, stakeholders involved in Synthetic data? In other words, what are the risks, if Synthetic data does not deliver successfully?
<--- Score

16. Are there any specific expectations or concerns about the Synthetic data team, Synthetic data itself?
<--- Score

17. Do you have/need 24-hour access to key personnel?
<--- Score

18. Are losses recognized in a timely manner?
<--- Score

19. Do you know what you need to know about Synthetic data?
<--- Score

20. Who else hopes to benefit from it?
<--- Score

21. Why the need?
<--- Score

22. How does it fit into your organizational needs and tasks?
<--- Score

23. What is the problem or issue?
<--- Score

24. What needs to be done?
<--- Score

25. What does Synthetic data success mean to the stakeholders?
<--- Score

26. Are you dealing with any of the same issues today as yesterday? What can you do about this?
<--- Score

27. Which issues are too important to ignore?
<--- Score

28. Is it clear when you think of the day ahead of you what activities and tasks you need to complete?
<--- Score

29. What are the Synthetic data resources needed?
<--- Score

30. What situation(s) led to this Synthetic data Self Assessment?
<--- Score

31. When a Synthetic data manager recognizes a

problem, what options are available?
<--- Score

32. Where do you need to exercise leadership?
<--- Score

33. Are there regulatory / compliance issues?
<--- Score

34. Will it solve real problems?
<--- Score

35. What needs to stay?
<--- Score

36. Have you identified your Synthetic data key performance indicators?
<--- Score

37. What Synthetic data events should you attend?
<--- Score

38. Are controls defined to recognize and contain problems?
<--- Score

39. What extra resources will you need?
<--- Score

40. What creative shifts do you need to take?
<--- Score

41. Which needs are not included or involved?
<--- Score

42. What do you need to start doing?

<--- Score

43. How do you identify subcontractor relationships?
<--- Score

44. What is the extent or complexity of the Synthetic data problem?
<--- Score

45. Think about the people you identified for your Synthetic data project and the project responsibilities you would assign to them, what kind of training do you think they would need to perform these responsibilities effectively?
<--- Score

46. What Synthetic data problem should be solved?
<--- Score

47. What is the problem and/or vulnerability?
<--- Score

48. Looking at each person individually – does every one have the qualities which are needed to work in this group?
<--- Score

49. How do you recognize an objection?
<--- Score

50. Who needs what information?
<--- Score

51. What are the stakeholder objectives to be achieved with Synthetic data?
<--- Score

52. How do you identify the kinds of information that you will need?
<--- Score

53. What do employees need in the short term?
<--- Score

54. Would you recognize a threat from the inside?
<--- Score

55. As a sponsor, customer or management, how important is it to meet goals, objectives?
<--- Score

56. What resources or support might you need?
<--- Score

57. Which information does the Synthetic data business case need to include?
<--- Score

58. Is the need for organizational change recognized?
<--- Score

59. How are you going to measure success?
<--- Score

60. Do you need different information or graphics?
<--- Score

61. How are the Synthetic data's objectives aligned to the group's overall stakeholder strategy?
<--- Score

62. What should be considered when identifying

available resources, constraints, and deadlines?
<--- Score

63. What is the recognized need?
<--- Score

64. What training and capacity building actions are needed to implement proposed reforms?
<--- Score

65. Does your organization need more Synthetic data education?
<--- Score

66. Who needs budgets?
<--- Score

67. What Synthetic data coordination do you need?
<--- Score

68. What are the clients issues and concerns?
<--- Score

69. What activities does the governance board need to consider?
<--- Score

70. Does the problem have ethical dimensions?
<--- Score

71. How many trainings, in total, are needed?
<--- Score

72. How do you recognize an Synthetic data objection?
<--- Score

73. What else needs to be measured?
<--- Score

74. What is the smallest subset of the problem you can usefully solve?
<--- Score

75. How do you assess your Synthetic data workforce capability and capacity needs, including skills, competencies, and staffing levels?
<--- Score

76. What are the expected benefits of Synthetic data to the stakeholder?
<--- Score

77. Does Synthetic data create potential expectations in other areas that need to be recognized and considered?
<--- Score

78. Why is this needed?
<--- Score

79. What would happen if Synthetic data weren't done?
<--- Score

80. How are training requirements identified?
<--- Score

81. What Synthetic data capabilities do you need?
<--- Score

82. Who are your key stakeholders who need to sign

off?
<--- Score

83. Who needs to know?
<--- Score

84. What are the timeframes required to resolve each of the issues/problems?
<--- Score

85. Whom do you really need or want to serve?
<--- Score

86. What prevents you from making the changes you know will make you a more effective Synthetic data leader?
<--- Score

87. Are there Synthetic data problems defined?
<--- Score

88. Consider your own Synthetic data project, what types of organizational problems do you think might be causing or affecting your problem, based on the work done so far?
<--- Score

89. Where is training needed?
<--- Score

90. What vendors make products that address the Synthetic data needs?
<--- Score

91. What problems are you facing and how do you consider Synthetic data will circumvent those

obstacles?
<--- Score

92. Who needs to know about Synthetic data?
<--- Score

93. Is the quality assurance team identified?
<--- Score

94. What is the Synthetic data problem definition? What do you need to resolve?
<--- Score

95. Is it needed?
<--- Score

96. Are your goals realistic? Do you need to redefine your problem? Perhaps the problem has changed or maybe you have reached your goal and need to set a new one?
<--- Score

97. What tools and technologies are needed for a custom Synthetic data project?
<--- Score

Add up total points for this section:
_____ = Total points for this section

Divided by: ______ (number of statements answered) = ______ Average score for this section

Transfer your score to the Synthetic data Index at the beginning of the Self-Assessment.

# CRITERION #2: DEFINE:

INTENT: Formulate the stakeholder problem. Define the problem, needs and objectives.

In my belief, the answer to this question is clearly defined:

5 Strongly Agree

4 Agree

3 Neutral

2 Disagree

1 Strongly Disagree

1. What are the requirements for audit information?
<--- Score

2. Is the Synthetic data scope manageable?
<--- Score

3. Who defines (or who defined) the rules and roles?
<--- Score

4. What information should you gather?
<--- Score

5. What are the tasks and definitions?
<--- Score

6. What is a worst-case scenario for losses?
<--- Score

7. What is the scope of the Synthetic data work?
<--- Score

8. How do you manage scope?
<--- Score

9. How was the 'as is' process map developed, reviewed, verified and validated?
<--- Score

10. Is Synthetic data linked to key stakeholder goals and objectives?
<--- Score

11. Does the team have regular meetings?
<--- Score

12. What Synthetic data services do you require?
<--- Score

13. What system do you use for gathering Synthetic data information?
<--- Score

14. How do you catch Synthetic data definition inconsistencies?
<--- Score

15. Has/have the customer(s) been identified?
<--- Score

16. Is there a Synthetic data management charter, including stakeholder case, problem and goal statements, scope, milestones, roles and responsibilities, communication plan?
<--- Score

17. What sort of initial information to gather?
<--- Score

18. How did the Synthetic data manager receive input to the development of a Synthetic data improvement plan and the estimated completion dates/times of each activity?
<--- Score

19. Has a team charter been developed and communicated?
<--- Score

20. What Synthetic data requirements should be gathered?
<--- Score

21. How do you gather the stories?
<--- Score

22. What are the dynamics of the communication plan?
<--- Score

23. What is the scope?
<--- Score

24. What is the context?
<--- Score

25. Has the direction changed at all during the course of Synthetic data? If so, when did it change and why?
<--- Score

26. What are the rough order estimates on cost savings/opportunities that Synthetic data brings?
<--- Score

27. How do you hand over Synthetic data context?
<--- Score

28. Who is gathering Synthetic data information?
<--- Score

29. What specifically is the problem? Where does it occur? When does it occur? What is its extent?
<--- Score

30. What are the compelling stakeholder reasons for embarking on Synthetic data?
<--- Score

31. Have the customer needs been translated into specific, measurable requirements? How?
<--- Score

32. Does the scope remain the same?
<--- Score

33. Is the Synthetic data scope complete and appropriately sized?
<--- Score

34. What are the boundaries of the scope? What is in bounds and what is not? What is the start point? What is the stop point?
<--- Score

35. Why are you doing Synthetic data and what is the scope?
<--- Score

36. How can the value of Synthetic data be defined?
<--- Score

37. How do you gather requirements?
<--- Score

38. How do you think the partners involved in Synthetic data would have defined success?
<--- Score

39. Do you have organizational privacy requirements?
<--- Score

40. Have all basic functions of Synthetic data been defined?
<--- Score

41. Has your scope been defined?
<--- Score

42. What is the worst case scenario?
<--- Score

43. How is the team tracking and documenting its work?
<--- Score

44. How will the Synthetic data team and the group measure complete success of Synthetic data?
<--- Score

45. When is the estimated completion date?
<--- Score

46. What customer feedback methods were used to solicit their input?
<--- Score

47. Are there different segments of customers?
<--- Score

48. Is Synthetic data currently on schedule according to the plan?
<--- Score

49. Is the current 'as is' process being followed? If not, what are the discrepancies?
<--- Score

50. What is the definition of success?
<--- Score

51. What are the Synthetic data tasks and definitions?
<--- Score

52. In what way can you redefine the criteria of choice clients have in your category in your favor?
<--- Score

53. What key stakeholder process output measure(s) does Synthetic data leverage and how?
<--- Score

54. What scope do you want your strategy to cover?
<--- Score

55. Is the scope of Synthetic data defined?
<--- Score

56. Is special Synthetic data user knowledge required?
<--- Score

57. What would be the goal or target for a Synthetic data's improvement team?
<--- Score

58. Do the problem and goal statements meet the SMART criteria (specific, measurable, attainable, relevant, and time-bound)?
<--- Score

59. What is in scope?
<--- Score

60. Will a Synthetic data production readiness review be required?
<--- Score

61. Who is gathering information?
<--- Score

62. Has anyone else (internal or external to the group) attempted to solve this problem or a similar one before? If so, what knowledge can be leveraged from these previous efforts?
<--- Score

63. Has the Synthetic data work been fairly and/

or equitably divided and delegated among team members who are qualified and capable to perform the work? Has everyone contributed?
<--- Score

64. Do you all define Synthetic data in the same way?
<--- Score

65. What are the core elements of the Synthetic data business case?
<--- Score

66. What information do you gather?
<--- Score

67. When is/was the Synthetic data start date?
<--- Score

68. Has the improvement team collected the 'voice of the customer' (obtained feedback – qualitative and quantitative)?
<--- Score

69. How have you defined all Synthetic data requirements first?
<--- Score

70. What happens if Synthetic data's scope changes?
<--- Score

71. Is there a completed SIPOC representation, describing the Suppliers, Inputs, Process, Outputs, and Customers?
<--- Score

72. How do you build the right business case?

<--- Score

73. Are customer(s) identified and segmented according to their different needs and requirements?
<--- Score

74. What gets examined?
<--- Score

75. What is the scope of the Synthetic data effort?
<--- Score

76. How would you define Synthetic data leadership?
<--- Score

77. How will variation in the actual durations of each activity be dealt with to ensure that the expected Synthetic data results are met?
<--- Score

78. Is the team equipped with available and reliable resources?
<--- Score

79. Is the team adequateiy staffed with the desired cross-functionality? If not, what additional resources are available to the team?
<--- Score

80. Has a high-level 'as is' process map been completed, verified and validated?
<--- Score

81. Are roles and responsibilities formally defined?
<--- Score

82. How does the Synthetic data manager ensure against scope creep?
<--- Score

83. What are the Roles and Responsibilities for each team member and its leadership? Where is this documented?
<--- Score

84. Do you have a Synthetic data success story or case study ready to tell and share?
<--- Score

85. How do you manage changes in Synthetic data requirements?
<--- Score

86. What are the record-keeping requirements of Synthetic data activities?
<--- Score

87. How do you keep key subject matter experts in the loop?
<--- Score

88. What intelligence can you gather?
<--- Score

89. Are the Synthetic data requirements complete?
<--- Score

90. Have specific policy objectives been defined?
<--- Score

91. Are accountability and ownership for Synthetic data clearly defined?

<--- Score

92. Who approved the Synthetic data scope?
<--- Score

93. What was the context?
<--- Score

94. If substitutes have been appointed, have they been briefed on the Synthetic data goals and received regular communications as to the progress to date?
<--- Score

95. Has everyone on the team, including the team leaders, been properly trained?
<--- Score

96. What sources do you use to gather information for a Synthetic data study?
<--- Score

97. Is there a clear Synthetic data case definition?
<--- Score

98. How are consistent Synthetic data definitions important?
<--- Score

99. Scope of sensitive information?
<--- Score

100. Is there regularly 100% attendance at the team meetings? If not, have appointed substitutes attended to preserve cross-functionality and full representation?
<--- Score

101. Has a project plan, Gantt chart, or similar been developed/completed?
<--- Score

102. What is the scope of Synthetic data?
<--- Score

103. Are all requirements met?
<--- Score

104. Have all of the relationships been defined properly?
<--- Score

105. Is the work to date meeting requirements?
<--- Score

106. Is there any additional Synthetic data definition of success?
<--- Score

107. What are (control) requirements for Synthetic data Information?
<--- Score

108. Are approval levels defined for contracts and supplements to contracts?
<--- Score

109. Are different versions of process maps needed to account for the different types of inputs?
<--- Score

110. Are there any constraints known that bear on the ability to perform Synthetic data work? How is the

team addressing them?
<--- Score

111. Are required metrics defined, what are they?
<--- Score

112. Will team members perform Synthetic data work when assigned and in a timely fashion?
<--- Score

113. What defines best in class?
<--- Score

114. When are meeting minutes sent out? Who is on the distribution list?
<--- Score

115. Is full participation by members in regularly held team meetings guaranteed?
<--- Score

116. Where can you gather more information?
<--- Score

117. Will team members regularly document their Synthetic data work?
<--- Score

118. What constraints exist that might impact the team?
<--- Score

119. How and when will the baselines be defined?
<--- Score

120. Is data collected and displayed to better

understand customer(s) critical needs and requirements.
<--- Score

121. What baselines are required to be defined and managed?
<--- Score

122. Are the Synthetic data requirements testable?
<--- Score

123. Who are the Synthetic data improvement team members, including Management Leads and Coaches?
<--- Score

124. Are resources adequate for the scope?
<--- Score

125. Is there a critical path to deliver Synthetic data results?
<--- Score

126. Is the improvement team aware of the different versions of a process: what they think it is vs. what it actually is vs. what it should be vs. what it could be?
<--- Score

127. Is there a completed, verified, and validated high-level 'as is' (not 'should be' or 'could be') stakeholder process map?
<--- Score

128. What is out-of-scope initially?
<--- Score

129. How often are the team meetings?
<--- Score

130. How do you gather Synthetic data requirements?
<--- Score

131. What scope to assess?
<--- Score

132. Is it clearly defined in and to your organization what you do?
<--- Score

133. What critical content must be communicated – who, what, when, where, and how?
<--- Score

134. Has a Synthetic data requirement not been met?
<--- Score

135. What knowledge or experience is required?
<--- Score

Add up total points for this section:
_____ = Total points for this section

Divided by: ______ (number of statements answered) = ______
Average score for this section

Transfer your score to the Synthetic data Index at the beginning of the Self-Assessment.

# CRITERION #3: MEASURE:

INTENT: Gather the correct data. Measure the current performance and evolution of the situation.

In my belief, the answer to this question is clearly defined:

5 Strongly Agree

4 Agree

3 Neutral

2 Disagree

1 Strongly Disagree

1. How will you measure success?
<--- Score

2. Are the measurements objective?
<--- Score

3. How do you measure success?
<--- Score

4. Are actual costs in line with budgeted costs?
<--- Score

5. Do you have an issue in getting priority?
<--- Score

6. What are the costs and benefits?
<--- Score

7. What are the estimated costs of proposed changes?
<--- Score

8. How do you prevent mis-estimating cost?
<--- Score

9. What is the cost of rework?
<--- Score

10. Are you able to realize any cost savings?
<--- Score

11. How do you measure efficient delivery of Synthetic data services?
<--- Score

12. How do you control the overall costs of your work processes?
<--- Score

13. What is the total cost related to deploying Synthetic data, including any consulting or professional services?
<--- Score

14. How do you aggregate measures across priorities?
<--- Score

15. When a disaster occurs, who gets priority?
<--- Score

16. Does the Synthetic data task fit the client's priorities?
<--- Score

17. Have you included everything in your Synthetic data cost models?
<--- Score

18. What does verifying compliance entail?
<--- Score

19. How frequently do you track Synthetic data measures?
<--- Score

20. How frequently do you verify your Synthetic data strategy?
<--- Score

21. Are supply costs steady or fluctuating?
<--- Score

22. Do you verify that corrective actions were taken?
<--- Score

23. How do you verify performance?
<--- Score

24. What are allowable costs?
<--- Score

25. What are the Synthetic data key cost drivers?

<--- Score

26. What users will be impacted?
<--- Score

27. What are the operational costs after Synthetic data deployment?
<--- Score

28. How will success or failure be measured?
<--- Score

29. Do you have any cost Synthetic data limitation requirements?
<--- Score

30. What does a Test Case verify?
<--- Score

31. What methods are feasible and acceptable to estimate the impact of reforms?
<--- Score

32. What are the costs of delaying Synthetic data action?
<--- Score

33. Have design-to-cost goals been established?
<--- Score

34. Will Synthetic data have an impact on current business continuity, disaster recovery processes and/or infrastructure?
<--- Score

35. What causes innovation to fail or succeed in your

organization?
<--- Score

36. How do you verify and validate the Synthetic data data?
<--- Score

37. Is the solution cost-effective?
<--- Score

38. What can be used to verify compliance?
<--- Score

39. Are you taking your company in the direction of better and revenue or cheaper and cost?
<--- Score

40. What causes extra work or rework?
<--- Score

41. How will your organization measure success?
<--- Score

42. Are there any easy-to-implement alternatives to Synthetic data? Sometimes other solutions are available that do not require the cost implications of a full-blown project?
<--- Score

43. What are your operating costs?
<--- Score

44. How sensitive must the Synthetic data strategy be to cost?
<--- Score

45. What is the cause of any Synthetic data gaps?
<--- Score

46. What are the current costs of the Synthetic data process?
<--- Score

47. Is the cost worth the Synthetic data effort ?
<--- Score

48. What harm might be caused?
<--- Score

49. How can you reduce the costs of obtaining inputs?
<--- Score

50. What are the Synthetic data investment costs?
<--- Score

51. Among the Synthetic data product and service cost to be estimated, which is considered hardest to estimate?
<--- Score

52. How will you measure your Synthetic data effectiveness?
<--- Score

53. How are measurements made?
<--- Score

54. At what cost?
<--- Score

55. Do the benefits outweigh the costs?
<--- Score

56. What are hidden Synthetic data quality costs?
<--- Score

57. How long to keep data and how to manage retention costs?
<--- Score

58. Is it possible to estimate the impact of unanticipated complexity such as wrong or failed assumptions, feedback, etcetera on proposed reforms?
<--- Score

59. What causes mismanagement?
<--- Score

60. What would be a real cause for concern?
<--- Score

61. How do you measure variability?
<--- Score

62. What could cause you to change course?
<--- Score

63. What details are required of the Synthetic data cost structure?
<--- Score

64. How to cause the change?
<--- Score

65. Was a business case (cost/benefit) developed?
<--- Score

66. Who is involved in verifying compliance?
<--- Score

67. What measurements are being captured?
<--- Score

68. What happens if cost savings do not materialize?
<--- Score

69. Are there competing Synthetic data priorities?
<--- Score

70. What disadvantage does this cause for the user?
<--- Score

71. Are missed Synthetic data opportunities costing your organization money?
<--- Score

72. What do people want to verify?
<--- Score

73. How do you verify your resources?
<--- Score

74. What drives O&M cost?
<--- Score

75. What is your decision requirements diagram?
<--- Score

76. How are costs allocated?
<--- Score

77. Where can you go to verify the info?
<--- Score

78. What could cause delays in the schedule?
<--- Score

79. Who should receive measurement reports?
<--- Score

80. Why do you expend time and effort to implement measurement, for whom?
<--- Score

81. What are the uncertainties surrounding estimates of impact?
<--- Score

**82. How does the upcoming avalanche of synthetic data impact data protection?**
<--- Score

83. Do you have a flow diagram of what happens?
<--- Score

84. Which measures and indicators matter?
<--- Score

85. What does your operating model cost?
<--- Score

86. Have you made assumptions about the shape of the future, particularly its impact on your customers and competitors?
<--- Score

87. Are Synthetic data vulnerabilities categorized and prioritized?
<--- Score

88. What measurements are possible, practicable and meaningful?
<--- Score

89. Do you aggressively reward and promote the people who have the biggest impact on creating excellent Synthetic data services/products?
<--- Score

90. How can you manage cost down?
<--- Score

91. What potential environmental factors impact the Synthetic data effort?
<--- Score

92. What would it cost to replace your technology?
<--- Score

93. How are you verifying it?
<--- Score

94. Are the units of measure consistent?
<--- Score

95. What causes investor action?
<--- Score

96. Are there measurements based on task performance?
<--- Score

97. What do you measure and why?
<--- Score

98. What are your customers expectations and measures?
<--- Score

99. Are the Synthetic data benefits worth its costs?
<--- Score

100. How do you verify if Synthetic data is built right?
<--- Score

101. Does management have the right priorities among projects?
<--- Score

102. Where is it measured?
<--- Score

103. Did you tackle the cause or the symptom?
<--- Score

104. Which Synthetic data impacts are significant?
<--- Score

105. How do you verify the authenticity of the data and information used?
<--- Score

106. What are the costs of reform?
<--- Score

107. Has a cost center been established?
<--- Score

108. How do you quantify and qualify impacts?
<--- Score

109. What is the Synthetic data business impact?
<--- Score

110. How will effects be measured?
<--- Score

111. How can you measure Synthetic data in a systematic way?
<--- Score

112. What evidence is there and what is measured?
<--- Score

113. How can you reduce costs?
<--- Score

114. What relevant entities could be measured?
<--- Score

115. How is the value delivered by Synthetic data being measured?
<--- Score

116. When should you bother with diagrams?
<--- Score

117. What tests verify requirements?
<--- Score

118. Are indirect costs charged to the Synthetic data program?
<--- Score

119. What are the costs?
<--- Score

120. Which costs should be taken into account?
<--- Score

121. How do you verify the Synthetic data requirements quality?
<--- Score

122. How will costs be allocated?
<--- Score

123. What are you verifying?
<--- Score

124. What are the types and number of measures to use?
<--- Score

125. Do you effectively measure and reward individual and team performance?
<--- Score

126. How do you measure lifecycle phases?
<--- Score

127. How do you verify and develop ideas and innovations?
<--- Score

128. How do you verify Synthetic data completeness and accuracy?
<--- Score

129. What is the total fixed cost?
<--- Score

130. How can you measure the performance?

<--- Score

131. Are you aware of what could cause a problem?
<--- Score

132. What is your Synthetic data quality cost segregation study?
<--- Score

133. Where is the cost?
<--- Score

134. What are your primary costs, revenues, assets?
<--- Score

135. What are your key Synthetic data organizational performance measures, including key short and longer-term financial measures?
<--- Score

136. How is progress measured?
<--- Score

137. How do your measurements capture actionable Synthetic data information for use in exceeding your customers expectations and securing your customers engagement?
<--- Score

Add up total points for this section:
_____ = Total points for this section

Divided by: ______ (number of statements answered) = ______
Average score for this section

Transfer your score to the Synthetic data Index at the beginning of the Self-Assessment.

# CRITERION #4: ANALYZE:

INTENT: Analyze causes, assumptions and hypotheses.

In my belief, the answer to this question is clearly defined:

5 Strongly Agree

4 Agree

3 Neutral

2 Disagree

1 Strongly Disagree

1. Which Synthetic data data should be retained?
<--- Score

2. Where is the data coming from to measure compliance?
<--- Score

3. What tools were used to generate the list of possible causes?
<--- Score

4. What Synthetic data data should be collected?
<--- Score

5. What is your organizations process which leads to recognition of value generation?
<--- Score

6. How much data can be collected in the given timeframe?
<--- Score

7. What will drive Synthetic data change?
<--- Score

8. Are you missing Synthetic data opportunities?
<--- Score

9. What is the complexity of the output produced?
<--- Score

**10. What is synthetic data and how can it complement good, clean data for AI to be successful?**
<--- Score

11. What conclusions were drawn from the team's data collection and analysis? How did the team reach these conclusions?
<--- Score

12. Do staff qualifications match your project?
<--- Score

13. What are the personnel training and qualifications required?

<--- Score

14. Who is involved in the management review process?
<--- Score

15. Is there an established change management process?
<--- Score

16. What is the cost of poor quality as supported by the team's analysis?
<--- Score

17. Who qualifies to gain access to data?
<--- Score

18. Who will facilitate the team and process?
<--- Score

19. What are your outputs?
<--- Score

**20. How do you create synthetic data?**
<--- Score

21. Who owns what data?
<--- Score

22. Think about some of the processes you undertake within your organization, which do you own?
<--- Score

23. What other organizational variables, such as reward systems or communication systems, affect the performance of this Synthetic data process?

<--- Score

24. What did the team gain from developing a sub-process map?
<--- Score

25. What are the Synthetic data business drivers?
<--- Score

26. What resources go in to get the desired output?
<--- Score

27. How is the data gathered?
<--- Score

28. How do you define collaboration and team output?
<--- Score

29. Is the suppliers process defined and controlled?
<--- Score

30. Are all team members qualified for all tasks?
<--- Score

31. How often will data be collected for measures?
<--- Score

32. Who is involved with workflow mapping?
<--- Score

33. What qualifications and skills do you need?
<--- Score

34. What Synthetic data data do you gather or use now?

<--- Score

**35. What is the difference between scrubbed and synthetic data?**
<--- Score

36. What process should you select for improvement?
<--- Score

37. Do quality systems drive continuous improvement?
<--- Score

38. Were there any improvement opportunities identified from the process analysis?
<--- Score

39. What were the crucial 'moments of truth' on the process map?
<--- Score

**40. Have experiments validating the concept been designed with synthetic data?**
<--- Score

41. How difficult is it to qualify what Synthetic data ROI is?
<--- Score

42. Have you defined which data is gathered how?
<--- Score

43. What qualifications do Synthetic data leaders need?
<--- Score

44. Where is Synthetic data data gathered?
<--- Score

45. How is data used for program management and improvement?
<--- Score

46. What is the oversight process?
<--- Score

47. What do you need to qualify?
<--- Score

48. How has the Synthetic data data been gathered?
<--- Score

49. What tools were used to narrow the list of possible causes?
<--- Score

50. How do you promote understanding that opportunity for improvement is not criticism of the status quo, or the people who created the status quo?
<--- Score

**51. Is synthetic data the enabler for wider AI adoption?**
<--- Score

52. What are the Synthetic data design outputs?
<--- Score

**53. Why do you need validation via synthetic data?**
<--- Score

54. Do your contracts/agreements contain data

security obligations?
<--- Score

55. A compounding model resolution with available relevant data can often provide insight towards a solution methodology; which Synthetic data models, tools and techniques are necessary?
<--- Score

**56. Why do you need training and validation via synthetic data?**
<--- Score

57. Do your employees have the opportunity to do what they do best everyday?
<--- Score

58. Is the final output clearly identified?
<--- Score

59. What are the necessary qualifications?
<--- Score

60. What Synthetic data metrics are outputs of the process?
<--- Score

**61. When is it safe to use synthetic data in supervised classification?**
<--- Score

62. What are your current levels and trends in key measures or indicators of Synthetic data product and process performance that are important to and directly serve your customers? How do these results compare with the performance of your competitors

and other organizations with similar offerings?
<--- Score

63. What are the disruptive Synthetic data technologies that enable your organization to radically change your business processes?
<--- Score

64. Who gets your output?
<--- Score

65. How do your work systems and key work processes relate to and capitalize on your core competencies?
<--- Score

66. How do you identify specific Synthetic data investment opportunities and emerging trends?
<--- Score

**67. How do you validate that synthetic data?**
<--- Score

68. What are the processes for audit reporting and management?
<--- Score

69. How do you implement and manage your work processes to ensure that they meet design requirements?
<--- Score

70. What successful thing are you doing today that may be blinding you to new growth opportunities?
<--- Score

71. What does the data say about the performance of the stakeholder process?
<--- Score

72. What quality tools were used to get through the analyze phase?
<--- Score

73. How is the way you as the leader think and process information affecting your organizational culture?
<--- Score

74. Do several people in different organizational units assist with the Synthetic data process?
<--- Score

75. What process improvements will be needed?
<--- Score

76. Are Synthetic data changes recognized early enough to be approved through the regular process?
<--- Score

77. How will the data be checked for quality?
<--- Score

**78. Why is it so hard for storage systems to unify data on a single platform?**
<--- Score

79. Are all staff in core Synthetic data subjects Highly Qualified?
<--- Score

**80. What are the conditions for the generation of synthetic data that improve classification?**

<--- Score

81. What qualifies as competition?
<--- Score

82. What are the revised rough estimates of the financial savings/opportunity for Synthetic data improvements?
<--- Score

**83. Have experiments validating the concept been performed with synthetic data?**
<--- Score

**84. How protective are synthetic data?**
<--- Score

85. Who will gather what data?
<--- Score

**86. Can the intruder use the data to find a match in the synthetic data file with high probability?**
<--- Score

87. Think about the functions involved in your Synthetic data project, what processes flow from these functions?
<--- Score

**88. What is the value of large synthetic datasets for conducting simulation studies?**
<--- Score

89. What internal processes need improvement?
<--- Score

90. How is Synthetic data data gathered?
<--- Score

91. How will the change process be managed?
<--- Score

92. How do you ensure that the Synthetic data opportunity is realistic?
<--- Score

93. What is the Value Stream Mapping?
<--- Score

94. What information qualified as important?
<--- Score

95. What training and qualifications will you need?
<--- Score

96. How will corresponding data be collected?
<--- Score

97. How do mission and objectives affect the Synthetic data processes of your organization?
<--- Score

98. What methods do you use to gather Synthetic data data?
<--- Score

99. Are your outputs consistent?
<--- Score

**100. Does the original data include anonymized or synthetic data?**
<--- Score

101. What are the best opportunities for value improvement?
<--- Score

102. What types of data do your Synthetic data indicators require?
<--- Score

103. How does the organization define, manage, and improve its Synthetic data processes?
<--- Score

104. What other jobs or tasks affect the performance of the steps in the Synthetic data process?
<--- Score

105. What controls do you have in place to protect data?
<--- Score

106. Should you invest in industry-recognized qualifications?
<--- Score

107. How will the Synthetic data data be captured?
<--- Score

108. How can risk management be tied procedurally to process elements?
<--- Score

109. What are your Synthetic data processes?
<--- Score

110. Where can you get qualified talent today?

<--- Score

111. What kind of crime could a potential new hire have committed that would not only not disqualify him/her from being hired by your organization, but would actually indicate that he/she might be a particularly good fit?
<--- Score

112. Is there a strict change management process?
<--- Score

113. An organizationally feasible system request is one that considers the mission, goals and objectives of the organization, key questions are: is the Synthetic data solution request practical and will it solve a problem or take advantage of an opportunity to achieve company goals?
<--- Score

114. How do you measure the operational performance of your key work systems and processes, including productivity, cycle time, and other appropriate measures of process effectiveness, efficiency, and innovation?
<--- Score

115. What, related to, Synthetic data processes does your organization outsource?
<--- Score

116. What were the financial benefits resulting from any 'ground fruit or low-hanging fruit' (quick fixes)?
<--- Score

117. Do you have the authority to produce the

output?
<--- Score

**118. Why is there a need for synthetic data?**
<--- Score

119. What are evaluation criteria for the output?
<--- Score

120. Is there any way to speed up the process?
<--- Score

121. What is the output?
<--- Score

122. How many input/output points does it require?
<--- Score

123. When should a process be art not science?
<--- Score

124. Record-keeping requirements flow from the records needed as inputs, outputs, controls and for transformation of a Synthetic data process, are the records needed as inputs to the Synthetic data process available?
<--- Score

125. Has data output been validated?
<--- Score

126. What Synthetic data data should be managed?
<--- Score

127. How do you use Synthetic data data and information to support organizational decision

making and innovation?
<--- Score

128. What is your organizations system for selecting qualified vendors?
<--- Score

129. How are outputs preserved and protected?
<--- Score

130. What data do you need to collect?
<--- Score

131. What output to create?
<--- Score

132. How is the Synthetic data Value Stream Mapping managed?
<--- Score

133. What qualifications are needed?
<--- Score

134. What systems/processes must you excel at?
<--- Score

135. What Synthetic data data will be collected?
<--- Score

136. What are your key performance measures or indicators and in-process measures for the control and improvement of your Synthetic data processes?
<--- Score

Add up total points for this section:
_____ = Total points for this section

Divided by: ______ (number of statements answered) = ______ Average score for this section

Transfer your score to the Synthetic data Index at the beginning of the Self-Assessment.

# CRITERION #5: IMPROVE:

INTENT: Develop a practical solution. Innovate, establish and test the solution and to measure the results.

In my belief, the answer to this question is clearly defined:

5 Strongly Agree

4 Agree

3 Neutral

2 Disagree

1 Strongly Disagree

1. If you could go back in time five years, what decision would you make differently? What is your best guess as to what decision you're making today you might regret five years from now?
<--- Score

2. How significant is the improvement in the eyes of the end user?
<--- Score

3. Who manages Synthetic data risk?
<--- Score

4. What resources are required for the improvement efforts?
<--- Score

5. Does a good decision guarantee a good outcome?
<--- Score

6. Are decisions made in a timely manner?
<--- Score

7. What area needs the greatest improvement?
<--- Score

8. How will you measure the results?
<--- Score

9. How is continuous improvement applied to risk management?
<--- Score

10. Do you cover the five essential competencies: Communication, Collaboration,Innovation, Adaptability, and Leadership that improve an organizations ability to leverage the new Synthetic data in a volatile global economy?
<--- Score

11. How risky is your organization?
<--- Score

12. Is any Synthetic data documentation required?
<--- Score

13. How do you measure risk?
<--- Score

14. What can you do to improve?
<--- Score

15. What is the magnitude of the improvements?
<--- Score

16. For decision problems, how do you develop a decision statement?
<--- Score

17. What does the 'should be' process map/design look like?
<--- Score

18. How can you improve Synthetic data?
<--- Score

19. What attendant changes will need to be made to ensure that the solution is successful?
<--- Score

20. Have you achieved Synthetic data improvements?
<--- Score

21. Were any criteria developed to assist the team in testing and evaluating potential solutions?
<--- Score

22. Explorations of the frontiers of Synthetic data will help you build influence, improve Synthetic data, optimize decision making, and sustain change, what is your approach?

<--- Score

23. Why improve in the first place?
<--- Score

24. How can skill-level changes improve Synthetic data?
<--- Score

25. How does your organization evaluate strategic Synthetic data success?
<--- Score

26. How can you better manage risk?
<--- Score

27. In the past few months, what is the smallest change you have made that has had the biggest positive result? What was it about that small change that produced the large return?
<--- Score

28. Who makes the Synthetic data decisions in your organization?
<--- Score

29. How do you link measurement and risk?
<--- Score

30. What are the affordable Synthetic data risks?
<--- Score

31. What strategies for Synthetic data improvement are successful?
<--- Score

32. Who will be using the results of the measurement activities?
<--- Score

33. Is there any other Synthetic data solution?
<--- Score

34. Is the implementation plan designed?
<--- Score

35. Risk Identification: What are the possible risk events your organization faces in relation to Synthetic data?
<--- Score

36. What communications are necessary to support the implementation of the solution?
<--- Score

37. How can the phases of Synthetic data development be identified?
<--- Score

38. Was a Synthetic data charter developed?
<--- Score

39. What is the team's contingency plan for potential problems occurring in implementation?
<--- Score

40. What practices helps your organization to develop its capacity to recognize patterns?
<--- Score

41. How do you keep improving Synthetic data?
<--- Score

42. Who will be responsible for documenting the Synthetic data requirements in detail?
<--- Score

43. What current systems have to be understood and/ or changed?
<--- Score

44. Which of the recognised risks out of all risks can be most likely transferred?
<--- Score

45. Who are the people involved in developing and implementing Synthetic data?
<--- Score

46. Are the most efficient solutions problem-specific?
<--- Score

47. How will you recognize and celebrate results?
<--- Score

48. What assumptions are made about the solution and approach?
<--- Score

49. What are the Synthetic data security risks?
<--- Score

50. What went well, what should change, what can improve?
<--- Score

51. Are you assessing Synthetic data and risk?
<--- Score

52. What Synthetic data improvements can be made?
<--- Score

53. What should a proof of concept or pilot accomplish?
<--- Score

54. Is the Synthetic data risk managed?
<--- Score

55. Does the goal represent a desired result that can be measured?
<--- Score

56. What are your current levels and trends in key measures or indicators of workforce and leader development?
<--- Score

57. Are risk management tasks balanced centrally and locally?
<--- Score

58. What is the risk?
<--- Score

59. Synthetic data risk decisions: whose call Is It?
<--- Score

60. What is the implementation plan?
<--- Score

61. What needs improvement? Why?
<--- Score

62. How do you decide how much to remunerate an employee?
<--- Score

63. What alternative responses are available to manage risk?
<--- Score

64. Who are the Synthetic data decision-makers?
<--- Score

65. Have you identified breakpoints and/or risk tolerances that will trigger broad consideration of a potential need for intervention or modification of strategy?
<--- Score

66. Risk events: what are the things that could go wrong?
<--- Score

67. Is pilot data collected and analyzed?
<--- Score

68. Is the Synthetic data documentation thorough?
<--- Score

69. How do you deal with Synthetic data risk?
<--- Score

70. Do you need to do a usability evaluation?
<--- Score

71. What were the underlying assumptions on the cost-benefit analysis?
<--- Score

72. How will you know that a change is an improvement?
<--- Score

73. How is knowledge sharing about risk management improved?
<--- Score

74. What tools do you use once you have decided on a Synthetic data strategy and more importantly how do you choose?
<--- Score

75. Is there a cost/benefit analysis of optimal solution(s)?
<--- Score

76. Do those selected for the Synthetic data team have a good general understanding of what Synthetic data is all about?
<--- Score

77. Risk factors: what are the characteristics of Synthetic data that make it risky?
<--- Score

78. What criteria will you use to assess your Synthetic data risks?
<--- Score

79. Who controls the risk?
<--- Score

80. Who are the Synthetic data decision makers?
<--- Score

81. Do vendor agreements bring new compliance risk ?
<--- Score

82. Is the optimal solution selected based on testing and analysis?
<--- Score

83. What is Synthetic data risk?
<--- Score

84. What tools were used to evaluate the potential solutions?
<--- Score

85. At what point will vulnerability assessments be performed once Synthetic data is put into production (e.g., ongoing Risk Management after implementation)?
<--- Score

86. How do you improve Synthetic data service perception, and satisfaction?
<--- Score

87. Is there a high likelihood that any recommendations will achieve their intended results?
<--- Score

88. What are the expected Synthetic data results?
<--- Score

89. What tools were most useful during the improve phase?
<--- Score

90. How scalable is your Synthetic data solution?
<--- Score

91. How do you improve your likelihood of success ?
<--- Score

92. What is the Synthetic data's sustainability risk?
<--- Score

93. Will the controls trigger any other risks?
<--- Score

94. How do you manage Synthetic data risk?
<--- Score

95. Who should make the Synthetic data decisions?
<--- Score

96. What actually has to improve and by how much?
<--- Score

97. Who manages supplier risk management in your organization?
<--- Score

98. What were the criteria for evaluating a Synthetic data pilot?
<--- Score

99. What tools were used to tap into the creativity and encourage 'outside the box' thinking?
<--- Score

100. Do you have the optimal project management team structure?

<--- Score

101. Is a solution implementation plan established, including schedule/work breakdown structure, resources, risk management plan, cost/budget, and control plan?
<--- Score

102. Who do you report Synthetic data results to?
<--- Score

103. How will you know that you have improved?
<--- Score

104. How do you measure progress and evaluate training effectiveness?
<--- Score

105. Who controls key decisions that will be made?
<--- Score

106. What error proofing will be done to address some of the discrepancies observed in the 'as is' process?
<--- Score

107. Which Synthetic data solution is appropriate?
<--- Score

108. How does the team improve its work?
<--- Score

109. Is the Synthetic data solution sustainable?
<--- Score

110. What to do with the results or outcomes of measurements?

<--- Score

111. How do you define the solutions' scope?
<--- Score

112. Is the scope clearly documented?
<--- Score

113. How do you measure improved Synthetic data service perception, and satisfaction?
<--- Score

114. Are events managed to resolution?
<--- Score

115. Is a contingency plan established?
<--- Score

116. How can you improve performance?
<--- Score

117. How do you mitigate Synthetic data risk?
<--- Score

118. Can you identify any significant risks or exposures to Synthetic data third- parties (vendors, service providers, alliance partners etc) that concern you?
<--- Score

119. What improvements have been achieved?
<--- Score

120. Was a pilot designed for the proposed solution(s)?
<--- Score

121. To what extent does management recognize Synthetic data as a tool to increase the results?
<--- Score

122. Are risk triggers captured?
<--- Score

123. How do you improve productivity?
<--- Score

124. Is Synthetic data documentation maintained?
<--- Score

125. What do you want to improve?
<--- Score

126. What risks do you need to manage?
<--- Score

127. Can you integrate quality management and risk management?
<--- Score

128. What is Synthetic data's impact on utilizing the best solution(s)?
<--- Score

129. Who will be responsible for making the decisions to include or exclude requested changes once Synthetic data is underway?
<--- Score

130. Do you combine technical expertise with business knowledge and Synthetic data Key topics include lifecycles, development approaches, requirements and how to make a business case?

<--- Score

131. Is there a small-scale pilot for proposed improvement(s)? What conclusions were drawn from the outcomes of a pilot?
<--- Score

132. What are the concrete Synthetic data results?
<--- Score

133. Are the key business and technology risks being managed?
<--- Score

134. Are procedures documented for managing Synthetic data risks?
<--- Score

135. What lessons, if any, from a pilot were incorporated into the design of the full-scale solution?
<--- Score

136. Is the measure of success for Synthetic data understandable to a variety of people?
<--- Score

137. Where do the Synthetic data decisions reside?
<--- Score

138. Would you develop a Synthetic data Communication Strategy?
<--- Score

139. For estimation problems, how do you develop an estimation statement?
<--- Score

140. Are the risks fully understood, reasonable and manageable?
<--- Score

Add up total points for this section:
_____ = Total points for this section

Divided by: ______ (number of statements answered) = ______ Average score for this section

Transfer your score to the Synthetic data Index at the beginning of the Self-Assessment.

# CRITERION #6: CONTROL:

INTENT: Implement the practical solution. Maintain the performance and correct possible complications.

In my belief, the answer to this question is clearly defined:

5 Strongly Agree

4 Agree

3 Neutral

2 Disagree

1 Strongly Disagree

1. Are operating procedures consistent?
<--- Score

2. Do the Synthetic data decisions you make today help people and the planet tomorrow?
<--- Score

3. Who has control over resources?
<--- Score

4. How will input, process, and output variables be checked to detect for sub-optimal conditions?
<--- Score

5. What is your plan to assess your security risks?
<--- Score

6. Can you adapt and adjust to changing Synthetic data situations?
<--- Score

7. Does the Synthetic data performance meet the customer's requirements?
<--- Score

8. What other systems, operations, processes, and infrastructures (hiring practices, staffing, training, incentives/rewards, metrics/dashboards/scorecards, etc.) need updates, additions, changes, or deletions in order to facilitate knowledge transfer and improvements?
<--- Score

9. Do you monitor the effectiveness of your Synthetic data activities?
<--- Score

10. Is there a Synthetic data Communication plan covering who needs to get what information when?
<--- Score

11. Are the planned controls in place?
<--- Score

12. Is knowledge gained on process shared and

institutionalized?
<--- Score

13. What is your theory of human motivation, and how does your compensation plan fit with that view?
<--- Score

14. What should the next improvement project be that is related to Synthetic data?
<--- Score

15. What are the key elements of your Synthetic data performance improvement system, including your evaluation, organizational learning, and innovation processes?
<--- Score

16. How do you encourage people to take control and responsibility?
<--- Score

17. What is the best design framework for Synthetic data organization now that, in a post industrial-age if the top-down, command and control model is no longer relevant?
<--- Score

18. Are there documented procedures?
<--- Score

19. How will the day-to-day responsibilities for monitoring and continual improvement be transferred from the improvement team to the process owner?
<--- Score

20. How do controls support value?
<--- Score

21. Will your goals reflect your program budget?
<--- Score

22. How likely is the current Synthetic data plan to come in on schedule or on budget?
<--- Score

23. What do you measure to verify effectiveness gains?
<--- Score

24. Who controls critical resources?
<--- Score

25. What are the critical parameters to watch?
<--- Score

26. What are the known security controls?
<--- Score

27. Is there a transfer of ownership and knowledge to process owner and process team tasked with the responsibilities.
<--- Score

28. Who is going to spread your message?
<--- Score

29. Are you measuring, monitoring and predicting Synthetic data activities to optimize operations and profitability, and enhancing outcomes?
<--- Score

30. How is change control managed?
<--- Score

31. How do your controls stack up?
<--- Score

32. Are suggested corrective/restorative actions indicated on the response plan for known causes to problems that might surface?
<--- Score

33. Is there a recommended audit plan for routine surveillance inspections of Synthetic data's gains?
<--- Score

34. Is there a standardized process?
<--- Score

35. Are the Synthetic data standards challenging?
<--- Score

36. Is reporting being used or needed?
<--- Score

37. How will the process owner verify improvement in present and future sigma levels, process capabilities?
<--- Score

38. Does Synthetic data appropriately measure and monitor risk?
<--- Score

39. What is the standard for acceptable Synthetic data performance?
<--- Score

40. Will any special training be provided for results interpretation?
<--- Score

41. Is a response plan in place for when the input, process, or output measures indicate an 'out-of-control' condition?
<--- Score

42. Who is the Synthetic data process owner?
<--- Score

43. How might the group capture best practices and lessons learned so as to leverage improvements?
<--- Score

44. What is the control/monitoring plan?
<--- Score

45. Are new process steps, standards, and documentation ingrained into normal operations?
<--- Score

46. How do you spread information?
<--- Score

47. How can you best use all of your knowledge repositories to enhance learning and sharing?
<--- Score

48. What are the performance and scale of the Synthetic data tools?
<--- Score

49. How do you plan for the cost of succession?
<--- Score

50. How widespread is its use?
<--- Score

51. Are controls in place and consistently applied?
<--- Score

52. Will existing staff require re-training, for example, to learn new business processes?
<--- Score

53. What quality tools were useful in the control phase?
<--- Score

54. What can you control?
<--- Score

55. Does a troubleshooting guide exist or is it needed?
<--- Score

56. Do you monitor the Synthetic data decisions made and fine tune them as they evolve?
<--- Score

57. Will the team be available to assist members in planning investigations?
<--- Score

58. Do the viable solutions scale to future needs?
<--- Score

59. Are documented procedures clear and easy to follow for the operators?
<--- Score

60. How will new or emerging customer needs/requirements be checked/communicated to orient the process toward meeting the new specifications and continually reducing variation?
<--- Score

61. Where do ideas that reach policy makers and planners as proposals for Synthetic data strengthening and reform actually originate?
<--- Score

62. How do senior leaders actions reflect a commitment to the organizations Synthetic data values?
<--- Score

63. Against what alternative is success being measured?
<--- Score

64. Can support from partners be adjusted?
<--- Score

65. Is there an action plan in case of emergencies?
<--- Score

66. Is a response plan established and deployed?
<--- Score

67. Implementation Planning: is a pilot needed to test the changes before a full roll out occurs?
<--- Score

68. Is there a documented and implemented monitoring plan?
<--- Score

69. What is the recommended frequency of auditing?
<--- Score

70. Has the Synthetic data value of standards been quantified?
<--- Score

71. Is there documentation that will support the successful operation of the improvement?
<--- Score

72. Have new or revised work instructions resulted?
<--- Score

73. How do you plan on providing proper recognition and disclosure of supporting companies?
<--- Score

74. Who will be in control?
<--- Score

75. What key inputs and outputs are being measured on an ongoing basis?
<--- Score

76. Has the improved process and its steps been standardized?
<--- Score

77. How do you monitor usage and cost?
<--- Score

78. What should you measure to verify efficiency gains?
<--- Score

79. In the case of a Synthetic data project, the criteria for the audit derive from implementation objectives, an audit of a Synthetic data project involves assessing whether the recommendations outlined for implementation have been met, can you track that any Synthetic data project is implemented as planned, and is it working?
<--- Score

80. Does job training on the documented procedures need to be part of the process team's education and training?
<--- Score

81. What Synthetic data standards are applicable?
<--- Score

82. Is the Synthetic data test/monitoring cost justified?
<--- Score

83. Are the planned controls working?
<--- Score

84. How is Synthetic data project cost planned, managed, monitored?
<--- Score

85. What do your reports reflect?
<--- Score

86. How will the process owner and team be able to hold the gains?
<--- Score

87. How will you measure your QA plan's effectiveness?
<--- Score

88. How do you select, collect, align, and integrate Synthetic data data and information for tracking daily operations and overall organizational performance, including progress relative to strategic objectives and action plans?
<--- Score

89. How do you establish and deploy modified action plans if circumstances require a shift in plans and rapid execution of new plans?
<--- Score

90. Is there a control plan in place for sustaining improvements (short and long-term)?
<--- Score

91. Does the response plan contain a definite closed loop continual improvement scheme (e.g., plan-do-check-act)?
<--- Score

92. What adjustments to the strategies are needed?
<--- Score

93. What do you stand for--and what are you against?
<--- Score

94. How will Synthetic data decisions be made and monitored?
<--- Score

95. You may have created your quality measures at a

time when you lacked resources, technology wasn't up to the required standard, or low service levels were the industry norm. Have those circumstances changed?
<--- Score

96. Is new knowledge gained imbedded in the response plan?
<--- Score

97. What other areas of the group might benefit from the Synthetic data team's improvements, knowledge, and learning?
<--- Score

98. How will report readings be checked to effectively monitor performance?
<--- Score

99. Are pertinent alerts monitored, analyzed and distributed to appropriate personnel?
<--- Score

Add up total points for this section:
_____ = Total points for this section

Divided by: ______ (number of statements answered) = ______ Average score for this section

Transfer your score to the Synthetic data Index at the beginning of the Self-Assessment.

# CRITERION #7: SUSTAIN:

INTENT: Retain the benefits.

In my belief, the answer to this question is clearly defined:

5 Strongly Agree

4 Agree

3 Neutral

2 Disagree

1 Strongly Disagree

1. How likely is it that a customer would recommend your company to a friend or colleague?
<--- Score

2. Is maximizing Synthetic data protection the same as minimizing Synthetic data loss?
<--- Score

3. What is a feasible sequencing of reform initiatives over time?
<--- Score

4. Who is responsible for ensuring appropriate resources (time, people and money) are allocated to Synthetic data?
<--- Score

5. What is the source of the strategies for Synthetic data strengthening and reform?
<--- Score

6. How do you maintain Synthetic data's Integrity?
<--- Score

7. Is a Synthetic data breakthrough on the horizon?
<--- Score

8. Do you have enough freaky customers in your portfolio pushing you to the limit day in and day out?
<--- Score

9. How do you accomplish your long range Synthetic data goals?
<--- Score

10. Why should people listen to you?
<--- Score

11. What is the purpose of Synthetic data in relation to the mission?
<--- Score

12. Is there any reason to believe the opposite of my current belief?
<--- Score

13. Are you relevant? Will you be relevant five years

from now? Ten?
<--- Score

14. If you had to leave your organization for a year and the only communication you could have with employees/colleagues was a single paragraph, what would you write?
<--- Score

15. Do you think you know, or do you know you know ?
<--- Score

16. Are all key stakeholders present at all Structured Walkthroughs?
<--- Score

17. What potential megatrends could make your business model obsolete?
<--- Score

18. Is there a work around that you can use?
<--- Score

19. In retrospect, of the projects that you pulled the plug on, what percent do you wish had been allowed to keep going, and what percent do you wish had ended earlier?
<--- Score

20. How do senior leaders deploy your organizations vision and values through your leadership system, to the workforce, to key suppliers and partners, and to customers and other stakeholders, as appropriate?
<--- Score

21. What is the funding source for this project?
<--- Score

22. How do you provide a safe environment -physically and emotionally?
<--- Score

23. Have benefits been optimized with all key stakeholders?
<--- Score

24. Who are four people whose careers you have enhanced?
<--- Score

25. Will it be accepted by users?
<--- Score

26. If there were zero limitations, what would you do differently?
<--- Score

27. Are your responses positive or negative?
<--- Score

28. If you got fired and a new hire took your place, what would she do different?
<--- Score

29. If no one would ever find out about your accomplishments, how would you lead differently?
<--- Score

30. If you were responsible for initiating and implementing major changes in your organization, what steps might you take to ensure acceptance of

those changes?
<--- Score

31. Why should you adopt a Synthetic data framework?
<--- Score

32. Are assumptions made in Synthetic data stated explicitly?
<--- Score

33. How do you assess the Synthetic data pitfalls that are inherent in implementing it?
<--- Score

34. Who are your customers?
<--- Score

35. Whose voice (department, ethnic group, women, older workers, etc) might you have missed hearing from in your company, and how might you amplify this voice to create positive momentum for your business?
<--- Score

36. What is effective Synthetic data?
<--- Score

37. Do you have an implicit bias for capital investments over people investments?
<--- Score

38. Who is responsible for Synthetic data?
<--- Score

39. Is your strategy driving your strategy? Or is the

way in which you allocate resources driving your strategy?
<--- Score

40. Who are the key stakeholders?
<--- Score

41. Who will provide the final approval of Synthetic data deliverables?
<--- Score

42. Are you making progress, and are you making progress as Synthetic data leaders?
<--- Score

43. What are the short and long-term Synthetic data goals?
<--- Score

44. How do you determine the key elements that affect Synthetic data workforce satisfaction, how are these elements determined for different workforce groups and segments?
<--- Score

45. Marketing budgets are tighter, consumers are more skeptical, and social media has changed forever the way we talk about Synthetic data, how do you gain traction?
<--- Score

46. Can you break it down?
<--- Score

47. How do you cross-sell and up-sell your Synthetic data success?

<--- Score

48. Can the schedule be done in the given time?
<--- Score

49. Why is Synthetic data important for you now?
<--- Score

50. What is the kind of project structure that would be appropriate for your Synthetic data project, should it be formal and complex, or can it be less formal and relatively simple?
<--- Score

51. Why do and why don't your customers like your organization?
<--- Score

52. What are the business goals Synthetic data is aiming to achieve?
<--- Score

53. How long will it take to change?
<--- Score

54. What Synthetic data skills are most important?
<--- Score

55. How do you engage the workforce, in addition to satisfying them?
<--- Score

56. What counts that you are not counting?
<--- Score

57. What are the usability implications of Synthetic

data actions?
<--- Score

58. Who, on the executive team or the board, has spoken to a customer recently?
<--- Score

59. What is the overall business strategy?
<--- Score

60. Have new benefits been realized?
<--- Score

61. Why will customers want to buy your organizations products/services?
<--- Score

62. What is the recommended frequency of auditing?
<--- Score

**63. Which members of a relatively unknown population should you target for retention?**
<--- Score

64. What would you recommend your friend do if he/she were facing this dilemma?
<--- Score

65. How do you manage Synthetic data Knowledge Management (KM)?
<--- Score

66. What management system can you use to leverage the Synthetic data experience, ideas, and concerns of the people closest to the work to be done?

<--- Score

67. What happens at your organization when people fail?
<--- Score

68. How do you create buy-in?
<--- Score

69. To whom do you add value?
<--- Score

70. Who will be responsible for deciding whether Synthetic data goes ahead or not after the initial investigations?
<--- Score

71. Is Synthetic data dependent on the successful delivery of a current project?
<--- Score

72. What are specific Synthetic data rules to follow?
<--- Score

73. Do you see more potential in people than they do in themselves?
<--- Score

74. Political -is anyone trying to undermine this project?
<--- Score

75. How do you ensure that implementations of Synthetic data products are done in a way that ensures safety?
<--- Score

76. How are you doing compared to your industry?
<--- Score

77. Who will manage the integration of tools?
<--- Score

78. What are the gaps in your knowledge and experience?
<--- Score

79. Were lessons learned captured and communicated?
<--- Score

80. What stupid rule would you most like to kill?
<--- Score

81. Are you maintaining a past–present–future perspective throughout the Synthetic data discussion?
<--- Score

82. What business benefits will Synthetic data goals deliver if achieved?
<--- Score

83. How do you keep the momentum going?
<--- Score

84. What must you excel at?
<--- Score

85. What could happen if you do not do it?
<--- Score

86. What happens when a new employee joins the organization?
<--- Score

87. How do you track customer value, profitability or financial return, organizational success, and sustainability?
<--- Score

88. Who do you want your customers to become?
<--- Score

89. Is Synthetic data realistic, or are you setting yourself up for failure?
<--- Score

90. Do you have the right capabilities and capacities?
<--- Score

91. How do you lead with Synthetic data in mind?
<--- Score

92. What relationships among Synthetic data trends do you perceive?
<--- Score

93. Who uses your product in ways you never expected?
<--- Score

94. What knowledge, skills and characteristics mark a good Synthetic data project manager?
<--- Score

95. What did you miss in the interview for the worst hire you ever made?

<--- Score

96. How will you insure seamless interoperability of Synthetic data moving forward?
<--- Score

97. What is your competitive advantage?
<--- Score

98. Do Synthetic data rules make a reasonable demand on a users capabilities?
<--- Score

99. Which models, tools and techniques are necessary?
<--- Score

100. What are the potential basics of Synthetic data fraud?
<--- Score

101. How do you foster the skills, knowledge, talents, attributes, and characteristics you want to have?
<--- Score

102. If your customer were your grandmother, would you tell her to buy what you're selling?
<--- Score

103. How will you ensure you get what you expected?
<--- Score

104. If you had to rebuild your organization without any traditional competitive advantages (i.e., no killer technology, promising research, innovative product/service delivery model, etcetera), how would your

people have to approach their work and collaborate together in order to create the necessary conditions for success?
<--- Score

105. If your company went out of business tomorrow, would anyone who doesn't get a paycheck here care?
<--- Score

106. What is an unauthorized commitment?
<--- Score

107. Did your employees make progress today?
<--- Score

108. Is a Synthetic data team work effort in place?
<--- Score

109. Who else should you help?
<--- Score

110. What is your BATNA (best alternative to a negotiated agreement)?
<--- Score

111. Are you changing as fast as the world around you?
<--- Score

112. How important is Synthetic data to the user organizations mission?
<--- Score

113. How can you negotiate Synthetic data successfully with a stubborn boss, an irate client, or a deceitful coworker?

<--- Score

114. Will there be any necessary staff changes (redundancies or new hires)?
<--- Score

115. Do you know what you are doing? And who do you call if you don't?
<--- Score

116. What unique value proposition (UVP) do you offer?
<--- Score

117. What are the top 3 things at the forefront of your Synthetic data agendas for the next 3 years?
<--- Score

118. What do we do when new problems arise?
<--- Score

119. Are you using a design thinking approach and integrating Innovation, Synthetic data Experience, and Brand Value?
<--- Score

120. When information truly is ubiquitous, when reach and connectivity are completely global, when computing resources are infinite, and when a whole new set of impossibilities are not only possible, but happening, what will that do to your business?
<--- Score

121. What information is critical to your organization that your executives are ignoring?
<--- Score

122. What is the big Synthetic data idea?
<--- Score

123. Whom among your colleagues do you trust, and for what?
<--- Score

124. Are the criteria for selecting recommendations stated?
<--- Score

125. What is the estimated value of the project?
<--- Score

126. Is the impact that Synthetic data has shown?
<--- Score

127. What may be the consequences for the performance of an organization if all stakeholders are not consulted regarding Synthetic data?
<--- Score

128. What is something you believe that nearly no one agrees with you on?
<--- Score

129. How will you motivate the stakeholders with the least vested interest?
<--- Score

130. What projects are going on in the organization today, and what resources are those projects using from the resource pools?
<--- Score

131. What is the range of capabilities?
<--- Score

132. Think of your Synthetic data project, what are the main functions?
<--- Score

133. Which Synthetic data goals are the most important?
<--- Score

134. How do you proactively clarify deliverables and Synthetic data quality expectations?
<--- Score

135. What was the last experiment you ran?
<--- Score

136. Are you / should you be revolutionary or evolutionary?
<--- Score

137. In a project to restructure Synthetic data outcomes, which stakeholders would you involve?
<--- Score

138. What happens if you do not have enough funding?
<--- Score

139. How can you become more high-tech but still be high touch?
<--- Score

140. What is your Synthetic data strategy?
<--- Score

141. What is the craziest thing you can do?
<--- Score

142. How do you govern and fulfill your societal responsibilities?
<--- Score

143. Which individuals, teams or departments will be involved in Synthetic data?
<--- Score

144. Do you say no to customers for no reason?
<--- Score

145. Are you satisfied with your current role? If not, what is missing from it?
<--- Score

146. Is there any existing Synthetic data governance structure?
<--- Score

147. What you are going to do to affect the numbers?
<--- Score

148. Do you have past Synthetic data successes?
<--- Score

149. Operational - will it work?
<--- Score

150. What threat is Synthetic data addressing?
<--- Score

151. Can you do all this work?

<--- Score

152. If you find that you havent accomplished one of the goals for one of the steps of the Synthetic data strategy, what will you do to fix it?
<--- Score

153. What will be the consequences to the stakeholder (financial, reputation etc) if Synthetic data does not go ahead or fails to deliver the objectives?
<--- Score

154. Where can you break convention?
<--- Score

155. What are the key enablers to make this Synthetic data move?
<--- Score

156. Do you feel that more should be done in the Synthetic data area?
<--- Score

157. What are the challenges?
<--- Score

158. Is it economical; do you have the time and money?
<--- Score

159. How do you transition from the baseline to the target?
<--- Score

160. Who do we want your customers to become?
<--- Score

161. Are there any activities that you can take off your to do list?
<--- Score

162. How do you make it meaningful in connecting Synthetic data with what users do day-to-day?
<--- Score

163. Who will determine interim and final deadlines?
<--- Score

164. Instead of going to current contacts for new ideas, what if you reconnected with dormant contacts--the people you used to know? If you were going reactivate a dormant tie, who would it be?
<--- Score

165. How is implementation research currently incorporated into each of your goals?
<--- Score

166. What have been your experiences in defining long range Synthetic data goals?
<--- Score

167. How much contingency will be available in the budget?
<--- Score

168. What role does communication play in the success or failure of a Synthetic data project?
<--- Score

169. How will you know that the Synthetic data project has been successful?

<--- Score

170. What is it like to work for you?
<--- Score

171. What are the long-term Synthetic data goals?
<--- Score

172. What does your signature ensure?
<--- Score

173. Who do you think the world wants your organization to be?
<--- Score

174. In the past year, what have you done (or could you have done) to increase the accurate perception of your company/brand as ethical and honest?
<--- Score

175. How do you deal with Synthetic data changes?
<--- Score

176. Who is the main stakeholder, with ultimate responsibility for driving Synthetic data forward?
<--- Score

177. What have you done to protect your business from competitive encroachment?
<--- Score

178. What is the overall talent health of your organization as a whole at senior levels, and for each organization reporting to a member of the Senior Leadership Team?
<--- Score

179. How does Synthetic data integrate with other stakeholder initiatives?
<--- Score

180. Why is it important to have senior management support for a Synthetic data project?
<--- Score

181. How do you stay inspired?
<--- Score

182. Are new benefits received and understood?
<--- Score

183. What is your question? Why?
<--- Score

184. What one word do you want to own in the minds of your customers, employees, and partners?
<--- Score

185. What are the success criteria that will indicate that Synthetic data objectives have been met and the benefits delivered?
<--- Score

186. What are the barriers to increased Synthetic data production?
<--- Score

187. Can you maintain your growth without detracting from the factors that have contributed to your success?
<--- Score

188. Why not do Synthetic data?
<--- Score

189. What trouble can you get into?
<--- Score

190. What are strategies for increasing support and reducing opposition?
<--- Score

191. Is the Synthetic data organization completing tasks effectively and efficiently?
<--- Score

192. How can you become the company that would put you out of business?
<--- Score

193. What is your formula for success in Synthetic data ?
<--- Score

194. Who is on the team?
<--- Score

195. How do customers see your organization?
<--- Score

196. Do you have the right people on the bus?
<--- Score

197. If you weren't already in this business, would you enter it today? And if not, what are you going to do about it?
<--- Score

198. What trophy do you want on your mantle?
<--- Score

199. Is your basic point _____ or _____?
<--- Score

200. Has implementation been effective in reaching specified objectives so far?
<--- Score

Add up total points for this section:
_____ = Total points for this section

Divided by: ______ (number of statements answered) = ______ Average score for this section

Transfer your score to the Synthetic data Index at the beginning of the Self-Assessment.

# Synthetic data and Managing Projects, Criteria for Project Managers:

# 1.0 Initiating Process Group: Synthetic data

1. What will be the pressing issues of tomorrow?

2. What do they need to know about the Synthetic data project?

3. Just how important is your work to the overall success of the Synthetic data project?

4. When will the Synthetic data project be done?

5. How can you make your needs known?

6. Were resources available as planned?

7. What input will you be required to provide the Synthetic data project team?

8. What will you do to minimize the impact should a risk event occur?

9. Do you understand the communication expectations for this Synthetic data project?

10. Do you understand the quality and control criteria that must be achieved for successful Synthetic data project completion?

11. How well did you do?

12. Did you use a contractor or vendor?

13. What were things that you did very well and want

to do the same again on the next Synthetic data project?

14. The Synthetic data project you are managing has nine stakeholders. How many channel of communications are there between corresponding stakeholders?

15. Who are the Synthetic data project stakeholders?

16. Were decisions made in a timely manner?

17. Who is funding the Synthetic data project?

18. What are the overarching issues of your organization?

19. How should needs be met?

# 1.1 Project Charter: Synthetic data

20. Will this replace an existing product?

21. Synthetic data project objective statement: what must the Synthetic data project do?

22. Market – identify products market, including whether it is outside of the objective: what is the purpose of the program or Synthetic data project?

23. How are Synthetic data projects different from operations?

24. Is it an improvement over existing products?

25. Synthetic data project background: what is the primary motivation for this Synthetic data project?

26. Why is it important?

27. What are the assigned resources?

28. Name and describe the elements that deal with providing the detail?

29. How much?

30. Why use a Synthetic data project charter?

31. Review the general mission What system will be affected by the improvement efforts?

32. Who will take notes, document decisions?

33. Assumptions: what factors, for planning purposes, are you considering to be true?

34. What goes into your Synthetic data project Charter?

35. How will you know that a change is an improvement?

36. Success determination factors: how will the success of the Synthetic data project be determined from the customers perspective?

37. Synthetic data project deliverables: what is the Synthetic data project going to produce?

38. Why have you chosen the aim you have set forth?

39. When is a charter needed?

## 1.2 Stakeholder Register: Synthetic data

40. What is the power of the stakeholder?

41. How will reports be created?

42. What are the major Synthetic data project milestones requiring communications or providing communications opportunities?

43. Is your organization ready for change?

44. Who are the stakeholders?

45. How much influence do they have on the Synthetic data project?

46. How big is the gap?

47. Who is managing stakeholder engagement?

48. What opportunities exist to provide communications?

49. Who wants to talk about Security?

50. How should employers make voices heard?

51. What & Why?

# 1.3 Stakeholder Analysis Matrix: Synthetic data

52. Marketing - reach, distribution, awareness?

53. Technology development and innovation?

54. What are the opportunities for communication?

55. How do rules, behaviors affect stakes?

56. How do customers express needs?

57. Would it be fair to say that cost is a controlling criteria?

58. Is there a clear description of the scope of practice of the Synthetic data projects educators?

59. Organizational Applicability?

60. Who holds positions of responsibility in interested organizations?

61. How are you predicting what future (work)loads will be?

62. How can you counter negative efforts?

63. What organizational arrangements are planned to ensure the Synthetic data project achieves its social development outcomes?

64. What is the relationship among stakeholders?

65. Why is it important to identify them?

66. If you can not fix it, how do you do it differently?

67. Market demand?

68. What mechanisms are proposed to monitor and measure Synthetic data project performance in terms of social development outcomes?

69. Are the interests in line with the program objectives?

70. New markets, vertical, horizontal?

71. Geographical, export, import?

# 2.0 Planning Process Group: Synthetic data

72. If action is called for, what form should it take?

73. How does activity resource estimation affect activity duration estimation?

74. Why is it important to determine activity sequencing on Synthetic data projects?

75. Does it make any difference if you are successful?

76. To what extent has the intervention strategy been adapted to the areas of intervention in which it is being implemented?

77. How well will the chosen processes produce the expected results?

78. Do the partners have sufficient financial capacity to keep up the benefits produced by the programme?

79. If task x starts two days late, what is the effect on the Synthetic data project end date?

80. Synthetic data project assessment; why did you do this Synthetic data project?

81. Did you read it correctly?

82. Did the program design/ implementation strategy adequately address the planning stage necessary to

set up structures, hire staff etc.?

83. To what extent is the program helping to influence your organizations policy framework?

84. How do you integrate Synthetic data project Planning with the Iterative/Evolutionary SDLC?

85. In which Synthetic data project management process group is the detailed Synthetic data project budget created?

86. What good practices or successful experiences or transferable examples have been identified?

87. If a risk event occurs, what will you do?

88. When will the Synthetic data project be done?

89. What types of differentiated effects are resulting from the Synthetic data project and to what extent?

90. Are the follow-up indicators relevant and do they meet the quality needed to measure the outputs and outcomes of the Synthetic data project?

# 2.1 Project Management Plan: Synthetic data

91. Are the existing and future without-plan conditions reasonable and appropriate?

92. What does management expect of PMs?

93. Is mitigation authorized or recommended?

94. Are calculations and results of analyzes essentially correct?

95. When is the Synthetic data project management plan created?

96. What is the business need?

97. Are the proposed Synthetic data project purposes different than a previously authorized Synthetic data project?

98. Is there anything you would now do differently on your Synthetic data project based on past experience?

99. Who is the sponsor?

100. Who is the Synthetic data project Manager?

101. Will you add a schedule and diagram?

102. What worked well?

103. Are alternatives safe, functional, constructible, economical, reasonable and sustainable?

104. What are the training needs?

105. What is the justification?

106. Why Change?

107. Who manages integration?

108. Are comparable cost estimates used for comparing, screening and selecting alternative plans, and has a reasonable cost estimate been developed for the recommended plan?

109. Are there any windfall benefits that would accrue to the Synthetic data project sponsor or other parties?

# 2.2 Scope Management Plan: Synthetic data

110. Does the business case include how the Synthetic data project aligns with your organizations strategic goals & objectives?

111. Are the Synthetic data project team members located locally to the users/stakeholders?

112. Are enough systems & user personnel assigned to the Synthetic data project?

113. Is there a formal process for updating the Synthetic data project baseline?

114. What weaknesses do you have?

115. Given the scope of the Synthetic data project, which criterion should be optimized?

116. Are schedule deliverables actually delivered?

117. Are the results of quality assurance reviews provided to affected groups & individuals?

118. Are meeting objectives identified for each meeting?

119. Have the procedures for identifying variances from estimates & adjusting the detailed work program been followed?

120. Has the scope management document been updated and distributed to help prevent scope creep?

121. Is documentation created for communication with the suppliers and Vendors?

122. Have you identified possible roadblocks?

123. How difficult will it be to do specific activities on this Synthetic data project?

124. Are decisions captured in a decisions log?

125. Were Synthetic data project team members involved in detailed estimating and scheduling?

126. Is stakeholder involvement adequate?

127. Do all stakeholders know how to access this repository and where to find the Synthetic data project documentation?

128. What are the risks that could significantly affect procuring consultant staff for the Synthetic data project?

## 2.3 Requirements Management Plan: Synthetic data

129. Will you perform a Requirements Risk assessment and develop a plan to deal with risks?

130. Are all the stakeholders ready for the transition into the user community?

131. Did you use declarative statements?

132. In case of software development; Should you have a test for each code module?

133. Who will do the reporting and to whom will reports be delivered?

134. Who is responsible for quantifying the Synthetic data project requirements?

135. What performance metrics will be used?

136. Did you distinguish the scope of work the contractor(s) will be required to do?

137. Did you avoid subjective, flowery or non-specific statements?

138. Who will finally present the work or product(s) for acceptance?

139. Could inaccurate or incomplete requirements in this Synthetic data project create a serious risk for the

business?

140. If it exists, where is it housed?

141. Do you understand the role that each stakeholder will play in the requirements process?

142. Are actual resources expenditures versus planned expenditures acceptable?

143. How do you know that you have done this right?

144. What information regarding the Synthetic data project requirements will be reported?

145. Is the change control process documented?

146. What went wrong?

147. How will you develop the schedule of requirements activities?

148. Will you document changes to requirements?

# 2.4 Requirements Documentation: Synthetic data

149. What will be the integration problems?

150. Is the requirement realistically testable?

151. Validity. does the system provide the functions which best support the customers needs?

152. What kind of entity is a problem ?

153. How will they be documented / shared?

154. Are there legal issues?

155. Is your business case still valid?

156. What is your Elevator Speech?

157. What are the attributes of a customer?

158. How does the proposed Synthetic data project contribute to the overall objectives of your organization?

159. Who provides requirements?

160. What marketing channels do you want to use: e-mail, letter or sms?

161. How linear / iterative is your Requirements Gathering process (or will it be)?

162. Can the requirement be changed without a large impact on other requirements?

163. Are there any requirements conflicts?

164. How will the proposed Synthetic data project help?

165. If applicable; are there issues linked with the fact that this is an offshore Synthetic data project?

166. Where do you define what is a customer, what are the attributes of customer?

167. What are the potential disadvantages/advantages?

168. How can you document system requirements?

## 2.5 Requirements Traceability Matrix: Synthetic data

169. Why do you manage scope?

170. What is the WBS?

171. How do you manage scope?

172. Is there a requirements traceability process in place?

173. How will it affect the stakeholders personally in career?

174. What are the chronologies, contingencies, consequences, criteria?

175. Do you have a clear understanding of all subcontracts in place?

176. How small is small enough?

177. Will you use a Requirements Traceability Matrix?

178. Describe the process for approving requirements so they can be added to the traceability matrix and Synthetic data project work can be performed. Will the Synthetic data project requirements become approved in writing?

179. What percentage of Synthetic data projects are producing traceability matrices between

requirements and other work products?

180. Why use a WBS?

# 2.6 Project Scope Statement: Synthetic data

181. Is there a Quality Assurance Plan documented and filed?

182. Have you been able to easily identify success criteria and create objective measurements for each of the Synthetic data project scopes goal statements?

183. If you were to write a list of what should not be included in the scope statement, what are the things that you would recommend be described as out-of-scope?

184. What actions will be taken to mitigate the risk?

185. Have you been able to thoroughly document the Synthetic data projects assumptions and constraints?

186. Which risks does the Synthetic data project focus on?

187. Are there specific processes you will use to evaluate and approve/reject changes?

188. Identify how your team and you will create the Synthetic data project scope statement and the work breakdown structure (WBS). Document how you will create the Synthetic data project scope statement and WBS, and make sure you answer the following questions: In defining Synthetic data project scope and the WBS, will you and your Synthetic data project

team be using methods defined by your organization, methods defined by the Synthetic data project management office (PMO), or other methods?

189. What are the major deliverables of the Synthetic data project?

190. Is the plan under configuration management?

191. Are there adequate Synthetic data project control systems?

192. If there is an independent oversight contractor, have they signed off on the Synthetic data project Plan?

193. What are the possible consequences should a risk come to occur?

194. Relevant - ask yourself can you get there; why are you doing this Synthetic data project?

195. Was planning completed before the Synthetic data project was initiated?

196. Write a brief purpose statement for this Synthetic data project. Include a business justification statement. What is the product of this Synthetic data project?

197. Did your Synthetic data project ask for this?

198. Do you anticipate new stakeholders joining the Synthetic data project over time?

199. Has the Synthetic data project scope statement

been reviewed as part of the baseline process?

200. What should you drop in order to add something new?

## 2.7 Assumption and Constraint Log: Synthetic data

201. Was the document/deliverable developed per the appropriate or required standards (for example, Institute of Electrical and Electronics Engineers standards)?

202. Have the scope, objectives, costs, benefits and impacts been communicated to all involved and/or impacted stakeholders and work groups?

203. When can log be discarded?

204. Does the document/deliverable meet all requirements (for example, statement of work) specific to this deliverable?

205. How can constraints be violated?

206. Have adequate resources been provided by management to ensure Synthetic data project success?

207. Do documented requirements exist for all critical components and areas, including technical, business, interfaces, performance, security and conversion requirements?

208. Are there standards for code development?

209. Are there nonconformance issues?

210. Should factors be unpredictable over time?

211. Diagrams and tables are included to account for complex concepts and increase overall readability?

212. What to do at recovery?

213. Contradictory information between different documents?

214. Have all necessary approvals been obtained?

215. Is the definition of the Synthetic data project scope clear; what needs to be accomplished?

216. What threats might prevent you from getting there?

217. Are there processes in place to ensure that all the terms and code concepts have been documented consistently?

218. Does a specific action and/or state that is known to violate security policy occur?

219. Have all involved stakeholders and work groups committed to the Synthetic data project?

220. What other teams / processes would be impacted by changes to the current process, and how?

## 2.8 Work Breakdown Structure: Synthetic data

221. How will you and your Synthetic data project team define the Synthetic data projects scope and work breakdown structure?

222. When would you develop a Work Breakdown Structure?

223. When do you stop?

224. Why would you develop a Work Breakdown Structure?

225. What has to be done?

226. Do you need another level?

227. How much detail?

228. When does it have to be done?

229. Who has to do it?

230. How big is a work-package?

231. Is the work breakdown structure (wbs) defined and is the scope of the Synthetic data project clear with assigned deliverable owners?

232. Where does it take place?

233. What is the probability of completing the Synthetic data project in less that xx days?

234. Is it still viable?

235. Can you make it?

236. Why is it useful?

237. How many levels?

## 2.9 WBS Dictionary: Synthetic data

238. Are the rates for allocating costs from each indirect cost pool to contracts updated as necessary to ensure a realistic monthly allocation of indirect costs without significant year-end adjustments?

239. Is cost and schedule performance measurement done in a consistent, systematic manner?

240. Does the cost accumulation system provide for summarization of indirect costs from the point of allocation to the contract total?

241. Is the work done on a work package level as described in the WBS dictionary?

242. Does the contractors system include procedures for measuring the performance of critical subcontractors?

243. Major functional areas of contract effort?

244. Performance to date and material commitment?

245. Should you include sub-activities?

246. Are meaningful indicators identified for use in measuring the status of cost and schedule performance?

247. Changes in the overhead pool and/or organization structures?

248. Are material costs reported within the same period as that in which BCWP is earned for that material?

249. Is each control account assigned to a single organizational element directly responsible for the work and identifiable to a single element of the CWBS?

250. Are current work performance indicators and goals relatable to original goals as modified by contractual changes, replanning, and reprogramming actions?

251. Are management actions taken to reduce indirect costs when there are significant adverse variances?

252. Are internal budgets for authorized, and not priced changes based on the contractors resource plan for accomplishing the work?

253. Can the contractor substantiate work package and planning package budgets?

254. Should you have a test for each code module?

255. Do the lines of authority for incurring indirect costs correspond to the lines of responsibility for management control of the same components of costs?

256. Are data elements reconcilable between internal summary reports and reports forwarded to us?

# 2.10 Schedule Management Plan: Synthetic data

257. Has a resource management plan been created?

258. Are vendor contract reports, reviews and visits conducted periodically?

259. Are Synthetic data project leaders committed to this Synthetic data project full time?

260. Are the schedule estimates reasonable given the Synthetic data project?

261. Has a sponsor been identified?

262. Synthetic data project definition & scope?

263. Does the Synthetic data project have a Quality Culture?

264. Are updated Synthetic data project time & resource estimates reasonable based on the current Synthetic data project stage?

265. Is there a formal set of procedures supporting Issues Management?

266. Were the budget estimates reasonable?

267. Are target dates established for each milestone deliverable?

268. Will the Synthetic data project sponsor be involved in preliminary schedule reviews?

269. How relevant is this attribute to this Synthetic data project or audit?

270. Where is the scheduling tool and who has access to it to view it?

271. Have all team members been part of identifying risks?

272. Are multiple estimation methods being employed?

273. Why time management?

274. Have adequate resources been provided by management to ensure Synthetic data project success?

275. Are the payment terms being followed?

## 2.11 Activity List: Synthetic data

276. What did not go as well?

277. How difficult will it be to do specific activities on this Synthetic data project?

278. Is there anything planned that does not need to be here?

279. In what sequence?

280. When do the individual activities need to start and finish?

281. What are you counting on?

282. What is your organizations history in doing similar activities?

283. What is the total time required to complete the Synthetic data project if no delays occur?

284. How do you determine the late start (LS) for each activity?

285. What are the critical bottleneck activities?

286. The wbs is developed as part of a joint planning session. and how do you know that youhave done this right?

287. Is infrastructure setup part of your Synthetic data project?

288. How much slack is available in the Synthetic data project?

289. How will it be performed?

290. What went well?

291. Who will perform the work?

292. What is the probability the Synthetic data project can be completed in xx weeks?

293. Where will it be performed?

## 2.12 Activity Attributes: Synthetic data

294. How do you manage time?

295. Where else does it apply?

296. Can more resources be added?

297. Resources to accomplish the work?

298. Have constraints been applied to the start and finish milestones for the phases?

299. What is missing?

300. Activity: what is In the Bag?

301. How else could the items be grouped?

302. Activity: fair or not fair?

303. Do you feel very comfortable with your prediction?

304. Time for overtime?

305. Which method produces the more accurate cost assignment?

306. How difficult will it be to complete specific activities on this Synthetic data project?

307. How many resources do you need to complete the work scope within a limit of X number of days?

308. Were there other ways you could have organized the data to achieve similar results?

309. Are the required resources available?

310. Would you consider either of corresponding activities an outlier?

311. How difficult will it be to do specific activities on this Synthetic data project?

312. Has management defined a definite timeframe for the turnaround or Synthetic data project window?

## 2.13 Milestone List: Synthetic data

313. How soon can the activity finish?

314. What background experience, skills, and strengths does the team bring to your organization?

315. Calculate how long can activity be delayed?

316. How late can each activity be finished and started?

317. What specific improvements did you make to the Synthetic data project proposal since the previous time?

318. Political effects?

319. What are your competitors vulnerabilities?

320. Reliability of data, plan predictability?

321. Describe your organizations strengths and core competencies. What factors will make your organization succeed?

322. Global influences?

323. Timescales, deadlines and pressures?

324. Competitive advantages?

325. How will the milestone be verified?

326. Information and research?

327. Which path is the critical path?

328. How will you get the word out to customers?

329. Vital contracts and partners?

330. What would happen if a delivery of material was one week late?

331. How late can the activity start?

## 2.14 Network Diagram: Synthetic data

332. Exercise: what is the probability that the Synthetic data project duration will exceed xx weeks?

333. If the Synthetic data project network diagram cannot change and you have extra personnel resources, what is the BEST thing to do?

334. How difficult will it be to do specific activities on this Synthetic data project?

335. Where do schedules come from?

336. Where do you schedule uncertainty time?

337. What job or jobs could run concurrently?

338. Planning: who, how long, what to do?

339. What is the probability of completing the Synthetic data project in less that xx days?

340. What are the Key Success Factors?

341. Will crashing x weeks return more in benefits than it costs?

342. What controls the start and finish of a job?

343. What activities must occur simultaneously with this activity?

344. How confident can you be in your milestone

dates and the delivery date?

345. What is the completion time?

346. What must be completed before an activity can be started?

347. What job or jobs follow it?

348. What is the lowest cost to complete this Synthetic data project in xx weeks?

349. If x is long, what would be the completion time if you break x into two parallel parts of y weeks and z weeks?

## 2.15 Activity Resource Requirements: Synthetic data

350. What is the Work Plan Standard?

351. What are constraints that you might find during the Human Resource Planning process?

352. Why do you do that?

353. How do you handle petty cash?

354. Do you use tools like decomposition and rolling-wave planning to produce the activity list and other outputs?

355. Other support in specific areas?

356. When does monitoring begin?

357. Anything else?

358. Which logical relationship does the PDM use most often?

359. How many signatures do you require on a check and does this match what is in your policy and procedures?

360. Are there unresolved issues that need to be addressed?

# 2.16 Resource Breakdown Structure: Synthetic data

361. Which resources should be in the resource pool?

362. What is Synthetic data project communication management?

363. What defines a successful Synthetic data project?

364. What is the difference between % Complete and % work?

365. How can this help you with team building?

366. Who delivers the information?

367. Who is allowed to perform which functions?

368. What is the primary purpose of the human resource plan?

369. How difficult will it be to do specific activities on this Synthetic data project?

370. Who will use the system?

371. The list could probably go on, but, the thing that you would most like to know is, How long & How much?

372. What is the number one predictor of a groups productivity?

373. Who is allowed to see what data about which resources?

374. What is the purpose of assigning and documenting responsibility?

375. Who needs what information?

## 2.17 Activity Duration Estimates: Synthetic data

376. How do functionality, system outputs, performance, reliability, and maintainability requirements affect quality planning?

377. If the optimiztic estimate for an activity is 12days, and the pessimistic estimate is 18days, what is the standard deviation of this activity?

378. How difficult will it be to do specific activities on this Synthetic data project?

379. What do corresponding sources say about Synthetic data project management?

380. Are team building activities completed to improve team performance?

381. Are activity dependencies identified?

382. Are measurement techniques employed to determine the potential impact of proposed changes?

383. Does a process exist for approving or rejecting changes?

384. Are expert judgment and historical information utilized to estimate activity duration?

385. Do procedures exist that identify when and how human resources are introduced and removed from

the Synthetic data project?

386. Calculate the expected duration for an activity that has a most likely time of 3, a pessimistic time of 10, and a optimiztic time of 2?

387. Which is correct?

388. Based on , if you need to shorten the duration of the Synthetic data project, what activity would you try to shorten?

389. How difficult will it be to complete specific activities on this Synthetic data project?

390. What should be done NEXT?

391. Who will promote it?

392. If Synthetic data project time and cost are not as important as the number of resources used each month, which is the BEST thing to do?

393. How does Synthetic data project management relate to other disciplines?

394. Find an example of a contract for information technology services. Analyze the key features of the contract. What type of contract was used and why?

# 2.18 Duration Estimating Worksheet: Synthetic data

395. What is an Average Synthetic data project?

396. How should ongoing costs be monitored to try to keep the Synthetic data project within budget?

397. What is next?

398. Science = process: remember the scientific method?

399. Do any colleagues have experience with your organization and/or RFPs?

400. Is the Synthetic data project responsive to community need?

401. When, then?

402. What utility impacts are there?

403. What is the total time required to complete the Synthetic data project if no delays occur?

404. Small or large Synthetic data project?

405. What info is needed?

406. How can the Synthetic data project be displayed graphically to better visualize the activities?

407. What went right?

408. Can the Synthetic data project be constructed as planned?

409. Will the Synthetic data project collaborate with the local community and leverage resources?

410. What work will be included in the Synthetic data project?

411. Why estimate time and cost?

412. What questions do you have?

413. Does the Synthetic data project provide innovative ways for stakeholders to overcome obstacles or deliver better outcomes?

414. Define the work as completely as possible. What work will be included in the Synthetic data project?

## 2.19 Project Schedule: Synthetic data

415. Meet requirements?

416. How do you know that youhave done this right?

417. How can you address that situation?

418. Is Synthetic data project work proceeding in accordance with the original Synthetic data project schedule?

419. Why is this particularly bad?

420. How do you manage Synthetic data project Risk?

421. Understand the constraints used in preparing the schedule. Are activities connected because logic dictates the order in which others occur?

422. Is the Synthetic data project schedule available for all Synthetic data project team members to review?

423. How do you use schedules?

424. Month Synthetic data project take?

425. Is the structure for tracking the Synthetic data project schedule well defined and assigned to a specific individual?

426. Was the Synthetic data project schedule reviewed by all stakeholders and formally accepted?

427. What is risk?

428. Have all Synthetic data project delays been adequately accounted for, communicated to all stakeholders and adjustments made in overall Synthetic data project schedule?

429. How effectively were issues able to be resolved without impacting the Synthetic data project Schedule or Budget?

430. If there are any qualifying green components to this Synthetic data project, what portion of the total Synthetic data project cost is green?

431. Does the condition or event threaten the Synthetic data projects objectives in any ways?

432. What documents, if any, will the subcontractor provide (eg Synthetic data project schedule, quality plan etc)?

## 2.20 Cost Management Plan: Synthetic data

433. Does the Synthetic data project have a Statement of Work?

434. Similar Synthetic data projects?

435. Are mitigation strategies identified?

436. Will the earned value reporting interface between time and cost management?

437. What would the life cycle costs be?

438. Is the Synthetic data project schedule available for all Synthetic data project team members to review?

439. Have activity relationships and interdependencies within tasks been adequately identified?

440. Have process improvement efforts been completed before requirements efforts begin?

441. Has the business need been clearly defined?

442. Are non-critical path items updated and agreed upon with the teams?

443. What is Synthetic data project cost management?

444. Schedule variances – how will schedule variances be identified and corrected?

445. How relevant is this attribute to this Synthetic data project or audit?

446. Are Synthetic data project team members committed fulltime?

447. Is there a formal process for updating the Synthetic data project baseline?

448. Are quality inspections and review activities listed in the Synthetic data project schedule(s)?

449. Are the key elements of a Synthetic data project Charter present?

450. Alignment to strategic goals & objectives?

451. Is there any form of automated support for Issues Management?

## 2.21 Activity Cost Estimates: Synthetic data

452. What were things that you did very well and want to do the same again on the next Synthetic data project?

453. Did the consultant work with local staff to develop local capacity?

454. What skill level is required to do the job?

455. What makes a good expected result statement?

456. Vac -variance at completion, how much over/ under budget do you expect to be?

457. Was the consultant knowledgeable about the program?

458. What is the Synthetic data projects sustainability strategy that will ensure Synthetic data project results will endure or be sustained?

459. Which contract type places the most risk on the seller?

460. What do you want to know about the stay to know if costs were inappropriately high or low?

461. Will you need to provide essential services information about activities?

462. How do you do activity recasts?

463. What is the activity inventory?

464. How do you treat administrative costs in the activity inventory?

465. Why do you manage cost?

466. How do you allocate indirect costs to activities?

467. Is there anything unique in this Synthetic data projects scope statement that will affect resources?

468. One way to define activities is to consider how organization employees describe jobs to families and friends. You basically want to know, What do you do?

469. Were the tasks or work products prepared by the consultant useful?

470. Were you satisfied with the work?

471. What is included in indirect cost being allocated?

## 2.22 Cost Estimating Worksheet: Synthetic data

472. Who is best positioned to know and assist in identifying corresponding factors?

473. What can be included?

474. Does the Synthetic data project provide innovative ways for stakeholders to overcome obstacles or deliver better outcomes?

475. Will the Synthetic data project collaborate with the local community and leverage resources?

476. What happens to any remaining funds not used?

477. How will the results be shared and to whom?

478. What will others want?

479. Is it feasible to establish a control group arrangement?

480. What costs are to be estimated?

481. Can a trend be established from historical performance data on the selected measure and are the criteria for using trend analysis or forecasting methods met?

482. What is the estimated labor cost today based upon this information?

483. Is the Synthetic data project responsive to community need?

484. What additional Synthetic data project(s) could be initiated as a result of this Synthetic data project?

485. Ask: are others positioned to know, are others credible, and will others cooperate?

486. What is the purpose of estimating?

487. Value pocket identification & quantification what are value pockets?

488. Identify the timeframe necessary to monitor progress and collect data to determine how the selected measure has changed?

## 2.23 Cost Baseline: Synthetic data

489. Have the actual milestone completion dates been compared to the approved schedule?

490. Are there contingencies or conditions related to the acceptance?

491. What is the consequence?

492. Has training and knowledge transfer of the operations organization been completed?

493. Should a more thorough impact analysis be conducted?

494. For what purpose ?

495. What deliverables come first?

496. How accurate do cost estimates need to be?

497. Does a process exist for establishing a cost baseline to measure Synthetic data project performance?

498. Does the suggested change request seem to represent a necessary enhancement to the product?

499. Escalation criteria met?

500. Are you asking management for something as a result of this update?

501. How difficult will it be to do specific tasks on the Synthetic data project?

502. Has the Synthetic data projected annual cost to operate and maintain the product(s) or service(s) been approved and funded?

503. Is there anything unique in this Synthetic data projects scope statement that will affect resources?

504. What strengths do you have?

505. Have all the product or service deliverables been accepted by the customer?

506. Are procedures defined by which the cost baseline may be changed?

## 2.24 Quality Management Plan: Synthetic data

507. How do you ensure that protocols are up to date?

508. How do senior leaders create an environment that encourages learning and innovation?

509. How do you measure?

510. Checking the completeness and appropriateness of the sampling and testing. Were the right locations/ samples tested for the right parameters?

511. How are calibration records kept?

512. How do you check in-coming sample material?

513. How is the information recorded?

514. Does the system design reflect the requirements?

515. Do you periodically review your data quality system to see that it is up to date and appropriate?

516. What field records are generated?

517. How does your organization ensure the quality, reliability, and user-friendliness of its hardware and software?

518. How relevant is this attribute to this Synthetic data project or audit?

519. What is the Difference Between a QMP and QAPP?

520. How does training support what is important to your organization and the individual?

521. Who is responsible for writing the qapp?

522. What are the established criteria that sampling / testing data are compared against?

523. Are you following the quality standards?

524. Results Available?

525. How does the material compare to a regulatory threshold?

## 2.25 Quality Metrics: Synthetic data

526. How do you calculate corresponding metrics?

527. How do you calculate such metrics?

528. Do the operators focus on determining; is there anything you need to worry about?

529. Was the overall quality better or worse than previous products?

530. Filter visualizations of interest?

531. When will the Final Guidance will be issued?

532. Did the team meet the Synthetic data project success criteria documented in the Quality Metrics Matrix?

533. How do you communicate results and findings to upper management?

534. If the defect rate during testing is substantially higher than that of the previous release (or a similar product), then ask: Did you plan for and actually improve testing effectiveness?

535. Are interface issues coordinated?

536. Can you correlate your quality metrics to profitability?

537. Product Availability ?

538. Can visual measures help you to filter visualizations of interest?

539. Was material distributed on time?

540. What metrics do you measure?

541. Are quality metrics defined?

542. Which report did you use to create the data you are submitting?

543. Has trace of defects been initiated?

544. How do you know if everyone is trying to improve the right things?

545. How effective are your security tests?

## 2.26 Process Improvement Plan: Synthetic data

546. What is the return on investment?

547. The motive is determined by asking, Why do you want to achieve this goal?

548. Why quality management?

549. To elicit goal statements, do you ask a question such as, What do you want to achieve?

550. Where do you focus?

551. Modeling current processes is great, and will you ever see a return on that investment?

552. What is the test-cycle concept?

553. Are you making progress on your improvement plan?

554. Everyone agrees on what process improvement is, right?

555. How do you manage quality?

556. Are you making progress on the goals?

557. Why do you want to achieve the goal?

558. Where are you now?

559. Are you meeting the quality standards?

560. What personnel are the sponsors for that initiative?

561. Purpose of goal: the motive is determined by asking, why do you want to achieve this goal?

562. Management commitment at all levels?

563. If a process improvement framework is being used, which elements will help the problems and goals listed?

## 2.27 Responsibility Assignment Matrix: Synthetic data

564. Is the anticipated (firm and potential) business base Synthetic data projected in a rational, consistent manner?

565. Evaluate the impact of schedule changes, work around, etc?

566. Cwbs elements to be subcontracted, with identification of subcontractors?

567. What do you need to implement earned value management?

568. What do you do when people do not respond?

569. Are significant decision points, constraints, and interfaces identified as key milestones?

570. Does the contractors system provide unit or lot costs when applicable?

571. Are all authorized tasks assigned to identified organizational elements?

572. Is data disseminated to the contractors management timely, accurate, and usable?

573. Is budgeted cost for work performed calculated in a manner consistent with the way work is planned?

574. What can you do to improve productivity?

575. Synthetic data projected economic escalation?

576. Are records maintained to show how undistributed budgets are controlled?

577. Is the entire contract planned in time-phased control accounts to the extent practicable?

578. Undistributed budgets, if any?

579. Are people encouraged to bring up issues?

580. What expertise is not available in your department?

581. Competencies and craftsmanship – what competencies are necessary and what level?

## 2.28 Roles and Responsibilities: Synthetic data

582. What are your major roles and responsibilities in the area of performance measurement and assessment?

583. Key conclusions and recommendations: Are conclusions and recommendations relevant and acceptable?

584. Be specific; avoid generalities. Thank you and great work alone are insufficient. What exactly do you appreciate and why?

585. Does the team have access to and ability to use data analysis tools?

586. Authority: what areas/Synthetic data projects in your work do you have the authority to decide upon and act on the already stated decisions?

587. Is there a training program in place for stakeholders covering expectations, roles and responsibilities and any addition knowledge others need to be good stakeholders?

588. Are governance roles and responsibilities documented?

589. What should you highlight for improvement?

590. Who is involved?

591. Are Synthetic data project team roles and responsibilities identified and documented?

592. Does your vision/mission support a culture of quality data?

593. Required skills, knowledge, experience?

594. What specific behaviors did you observe?

595. What is working well within your organizations performance management system?

596. Do the values and practices inherent in the culture of your organization foster or hinder the process?

597. What expectations were met?

598. How well did the Synthetic data project Team understand the expectations of specific roles and responsibilities?

599. Once the responsibilities are defined for the Synthetic data project, have the deliverables, roles and responsibilities been clearly communicated to every participant?

600. To decide whether to use a quality measurement, ask how will you know when it is achieved?

## 2.29 Human Resource Management Plan: Synthetic data

601. Are risk triggers captured?

602. Based on your Synthetic data project communication management plan, what worked well?

603. Has a quality assurance plan been developed for the Synthetic data project?

604. Is the communication plan being followed?

605. Are risk oriented checklists used during risk identification?

606. Does the schedule include Synthetic data project management time and change request analysis time?

607. Is pert / critical path or equivalent methodology being used?

608. What were things that you need to improve?

609. What talent is needed?

610. List roles. what commitments have been made?

611. What is the boss?

612. Are written status reports provided on a designated frequent basis?

613. Are the Synthetic data project plans updated on a frequent basis?

614. Is the current culture aligned with the vision, mission, and values of the department?

615. Was your organizations estimating methodology being used and followed?

616. Have all documents been archived in a Synthetic data project repository for each release?

## 2.30 Communications Management Plan: Synthetic data

617. Is there an important stakeholder who is actively opposed and will not receive messages?

618. Why is stakeholder engagement important?

619. Will messages be directly related to the release strategy or phases of the Synthetic data project?

620. Why do you manage communications?

621. Is the stakeholder role recognized by your organization?

622. Who have you worked with in past, similar initiatives?

623. How much time does it take to do it?

624. Which stakeholders are thought leaders, influences, or early adopters?

625. Timing: when do the effects of the communication take place?

626. Who to learn from?

627. What is the stakeholders level of authority?

628. Are others needed?

629. How did the term stakeholder originate?

630. Why manage stakeholders?

631. Do you prepare stakeholder engagement plans?

632. Do you then often overlook a key stakeholder or stakeholder group?

633. Do you have members of your team responsible for certain stakeholders?

634. Are there potential barriers between the team and the stakeholder?

635. Who is responsible?

## 2.31 Risk Management Plan: Synthetic data

636. Methodology: how will risk management be performed on this Synthetic data project?

637. Number of users of the product?

638. Where do risks appear in the business phases?

639. For software; does the software interface with new or unproven hardware or unproven vendor products?

640. How do you manage Synthetic data project Risk?

641. Are flexibility and reuse paramount?

642. Are requirements fully understood by the software engineering team and customers?

643. Are enough people available?

644. How well were you able to manage your risk before?

645. Workarounds are determined during which step of risk management?

646. Can it be changed quickly?

647. Do the people have the right combinations of skills?

648. Is the process being followed?

649. Technology risk: is the Synthetic data project technically feasible?

650. What risks are necessary to achieve success?

651. Does the Synthetic data project team have experience with the technology to be implemented?

652. How are risk analvsis and prioritization performed?

653. Do you train all developers in the process?

654. Have customers been involved fully in the definition of requirements?

655. Are you on schedule?

## 2.32 Risk Register: Synthetic data

656. What are your key risks/show istoppers and what is being done to manage them?

657. Schedule impact/severity estimated range (workdays) assume the event happens, what is the potential impact?

658. Financial risk -can your organization afford to undertake the Synthetic data project?

659. Budget and schedule: what are the estimated costs and schedules for performing risk-related activities?

660. Do you require further engagement?

661. User involvement: do you have the right users?

662. Technology risk -is the Synthetic data project technically feasible?

663. What is your current and future risk profile?

664. What would the impact to the Synthetic data project objectives be should the risk arise?

665. What is the probability and impact of the risk occurring?

666. Risk documentation: what reporting formats and processes will be used for risk management activities?

667. When is it going to be done?

668. Cost/benefit – how much will the proposed mitigations cost and how does this cost compare with the potential cost of the risk event/situation should it occur?

669. Who is going to do it?

670. How are risks graded?

671. Assume the risk event or situation happens, what would the impact be?

672. Is further information required before making a decision?

673. What could prevent you delivering on the strategic program objectives and what is being done to mitigate corresponding issues?

674. Market risk -will the new service or product be useful to your organization or marketable to others?

675. Recovery actions - planned actions taken once a risk has occurred to allow you to move on. What should you do after?

## 2.33 Probability and Impact Assessment: Synthetic data

676. Why has this particular mode of contracting been chosen?

677. Can you stabilize dynamic risk factors?

678. How will economic events and trends likely affect the Synthetic data project?

679. What is the Synthetic data project managers level of commitment and professionalism?

680. Is the technology to be built new to your organization?

681. What are its business ethics?

682. How well is the risk understood?

683. Monitoring of the overall Synthetic data project status – are there any changes in the Synthetic data project that can effect and cause new possible risks?

684. How are the local factors going to affect the absorption?

685. Do the requirements require the creation of new algorithms?

686. How is the risk management process used in practice?

687. Should the risk be taken at all?

688. Do you have a consistent repeatable process that is actually used?

689. Does the software engineering team have the right mix of skills?

690. What is the experience (performance, attitude, business ethics, etc.) in the past with contractors?

691. What will be the environmental impact of the Synthetic data project?

692. What is the probability of the risk occurring?

693. Can you avoid altogether some things that might go wrong?

694. What are the uncertainties associated with the technology selected for the Synthetic data project?

## 2.34 Probability and Impact Matrix: Synthetic data

695. How is the Synthetic data project going to be managed?

696. What should be the gestation period for the Synthetic data project with this technology?

697. What are ways to measure and evaluate risks?

698. Is security a central objective?

699. How can you understand and diagnose risks and identify sources?

700. What are the probable external agencies to act as Synthetic data project manager?

701. What will be cost of redeployment of the personnel?

702. What are the methods to deal with risks?

703. Are staff committed for the duration of the Synthetic data project?

704. What things are likely to change?

705. Are there alternative opinions/solutions/ processes you should explore?

706. What is the level of commitment and

professionalism?

707. How would you assess the risk management process in the Synthetic data project?

708. Does the customer have a solid idea of what is required?

709. How much is the probability of the risk occurring?

710. How would you suggest monitoring for risk transition indicators?

711. Does the customer understand the software process?

712. What should be done with risks on the watch list?

713. What is the political situation at present?

## 2.35 Risk Data Sheet: Synthetic data

714. What actions can be taken to eliminate or remove risk?

715. How do you handle product safely?

716. Is the data sufficiently specified in terms of the type of failure being analyzed, and its frequency or probability?

717. Whom do you serve (customers)?

718. How reliable is the data source?

719. What are your core values?

720. What was measured?

721. What are you trying to achieve (Objectives)?

722. What will be the consequences if the risk happens?

723. Has the most cost-effective solution been chosen?

724. What is the environment within which you operate (social trends, economic, community values, broad based participation, national directions etc.)?

725. What is the likelihood of it happening?

726. What if client refuses?

727. Has a sensitivity analysis been carried out?

728. How can it happen?

729. How can hazards be reduced?

730. What can you do?

731. Who has a vested interest in how you perform as your organization (our stakeholders)?

## 2.36 Procurement Management Plan: Synthetic data

732. Is there a set of procedures to capture, analyze and act on quality metrics?

733. Has Synthetic data project success criteria been defined?

734. Has a provision been made to reassess Synthetic data project risks at various Synthetic data project stages?

735. Have reserves been created to address risks?

736. Is there a procurement management plan in place?

737. Have Synthetic data project management standards and procedures been identified / established and documented?

738. Is the structure for tracking the Synthetic data project schedule well defined and assigned to a specific individual?

739. Are decisions made in a timely manner?

740. Is there a requirements change management processes in place?

741. Does a documented Synthetic data project organizational policy & plan (i.e. governance model)

exist?

742. Are the quality tools and methods identified in the Quality Plan appropriate to the Synthetic data project?

743. Have Synthetic data project team accountabilities & responsibilities been clearly defined?

744. Were escalated issues resolved promptly?

745. What areas are overlooked on this Synthetic data project?

746. Are the budget estimates reasonable?

# 2.37 Source Selection Criteria: Synthetic data

747. Does the evaluation of any change include an impact analysis; how will the change affect the scope, time, cost, and quality of the goods or services being provided?

748. What is price analysis and when should it be performed?

749. How are clarifications and communications appropriately used?

750. When is it appropriate to issue a DRFP?

751. When is it appropriate to issue a Draft Request for Proposal (DRFP)?

752. When should debriefings be held and how should they be scheduled?

753. Do you have designated specific forms or worksheets?

754. Has all proposal data been loaded?

755. How much past performance information should be requested?

756. What does a sample rating scale look like?

757. What are open book debriefings?

758. Who is entitled to a debriefing?

759. How is past performance evaluated?

760. Do you ensure you evaluate what you asked for, not what you want to see or expect to see?

761. How and when do you enter into Synthetic data project Procurement Management?

762. When is it appropriate to conduct a preproposal conference?

763. What are the most common types of rating systems?

764. Who must be notified?

765. What is the last item a Synthetic data project manager must do to finalize Synthetic data project close-out?

766. When and what information can be considered with offerors regarding past performance?

## 2.38 Stakeholder Management Plan: Synthetic data

767. What is positive about the current process?

768. Are issues raised, assessed, actioned, and resolved in a timely and efficient manner?

769. What potential impact does the stakeholder have on the Synthetic data project?

770. How will you engage this stakeholder and gain commitment?

771. At what point will the Synthetic data project be closed and what will be done to formally close the Synthetic data project?

772. Does the Synthetic data project have a Statement of Work?

773. What is meant by managing the triple constraint?

774. Are all resource assumptions documented?

775. Are best practices and metrics employed to identify issues, progress, performance, etc.?

776. Have Synthetic data project team accountabilities & responsibilities been clearly defined?

777. Are changes in deliverable commitments agreed to by all affected groups & individuals?

778. What has to be purchased?

779. Were Synthetic data project team members involved in detailed estimating and scheduling?

# 2.39 Change Management Plan: Synthetic data

780. What method and medium would you use to announce a message?

781. Which relationships will change?

782. What roles within your organization are affected, and how?

783. Is there a need for new relationships to be built?

784. Where do you want to be?

785. Readiness -what is a successful end state?

786. Do you need new systems?

787. Is a training information sheet available?

788. Have the systems been configured and tested?

789. Has an information & communications plan been developed?

790. How will you deal with anger about the restricting of communications due to confidentiality considerations?

791. Who might present the most resistance?

792. Will all field readiness criteria have been

practically met prior to training roll-out?

793. What new competencies will be required for the roles?

794. Who will do the training?

795. Has the target training audience been identified and nominated?

796. How might they respond to the message and if the response may be negative or open to misinterpretation, what else needs to be said?

797. Are work location changes required?

798. What new behaviours are required?

799. What are the essentials of the message?

# 3.0 Executing Process Group: Synthetic data

800. Have operating capacities been created and/or reinforced in partners?

801. What are the main types of goods and services being outsourced?

802. What are the Synthetic data project management deliverables of each process group?

803. In what way has the program come up with innovative measures for problem-solving?

804. Do Synthetic data project managers understand your organizational context for Synthetic data projects?

805. Will additional funds be needed for hardware or software?

806. How could stakeholders negatively impact your Synthetic data project?

807. Who are the Synthetic data project stakeholders?

808. What is the difference between using brainstorming and the Delphi technique for risk identification?

809. Mitigate. what will you do to minimize the impact should a risk event occur?

810. What were things that you did very well and want to do the same again on the next Synthetic data project?

811. Do your results resemble a normal distribution?

812. Do schedule issues conflicts?

813. What are the main types of contracts if you do decide to outsource?

814. Who will provide training?

815. How can you use Microsoft Synthetic data project and Excel to assist in Synthetic data project risk management?

816. What are the critical steps involved with strategy mapping?

817. How does a Synthetic data project life cycle differ from a product life cycle?

818. What type of information goes in the quality assurance plan?

## 3.1 Team Member Status Report: Synthetic data

819. How much risk is involved?

820. How can you make it practical?

821. How it is to be done?

822. How will resource planning be done?

823. Are the attitudes of staff regarding Synthetic data project work improving?

824. Why is it to be done?

825. How does this product, good, or service meet the needs of the Synthetic data project and your organization as a whole?

826. The problem with Reward & Recognition Programs is that the truly deserving people all too often get left out. How can you make it practical?

827. Do you have an Enterprise Synthetic data project Management Office (EPMO)?

828. Are the products of your organizations Synthetic data projects meeting customers objectives?

829. Does every department have to have a Synthetic data project Manager on staff?

830. What specific interest groups do you have in place?

831. Are your organizations Synthetic data projects more successful over time?

832. Is there evidence that staff is taking a more professional approach toward management of your organizations Synthetic data projects?

833. Does your organization have the means (staff, money, contract, etc.) to produce or to acquire the product, good, or service?

834. Does the product, good, or service already exist within your organization?

835. When a teams productivity and success depend on collaboration and the efficient flow of information, what generally fails them?

836. What is to be done?

837. Will the staff do training or is that done by a third party?

## 3.2 Change Request: Synthetic data

838. Where do changes come from?

839. When to submit a change request?

840. What are the Impacts to your organization?

841. How is the change documented (format, content, storage)?

842. Can static requirements change attributes like the size of the change be used to predict reliability in execution?

843. Screen shots or attachments included in a Change Request?

844. Are there requirements attributes that are strongly related to the complexity and size?

845. What are the requirements for urgent changes?

846. Has your address changed?

847. What is a Change Request Form?

848. Since there are no change requests in your Synthetic data project at this point, what must you have before you begin?

849. What can be filed?

850. Who has responsibility for approving and ranking

changes?

851. Is it feasible to use requirements attributes as predictors of reliability?

852. Who is communicating the change?

853. Who can suggest changes?

854. What should be regulated in a change control operating instruction?

855. What needs to be communicated?

856. Who is responsible for the implementation and monitoring of all measures?

857. Why were your requested changes rejected or not made?

## 3.3 Change Log: Synthetic data

858. Is the change request open, closed or pending?

859. Is the change backward compatible without limitations?

860. Is this a mandatory replacement?

861. How does this relate to the standards developed for specific business processes?

862. Do the described changes impact on the integrity or security of the system?

863. Will the Synthetic data project fail if the change request is not executed?

864. Is the submitted change a new change or a modification of a previously approved change?

865. When was the request submitted?

866. How does this change affect scope?

867. Is the change request within Synthetic data project scope?

868. Is the requested change request a result of changes in other Synthetic data project(s)?

869. Who initiated the change request?

870. When was the request approved?

871. Does the suggested change request represent a desired enhancement to the products functionality?

872. How does this change affect the timeline of the schedule?

## 3.4 Decision Log: Synthetic data

873. What is the average size of your matters in an applicable measurement?

874. What are the cost implications?

875. What alternatives/risks were considered?

876. How do you define success?

877. With whom was the decision shared or considered?

878. Which variables make a critical difference?

879. How consolidated and comprehensive a story can you tell by capturing currently available incident data in a central location and through a log of key decisions during an incident?

880. Decision-making process; how will the team make decisions?

881. At what point in time does loss become unacceptable?

882. How does the use a Decision Support System influence the strategies/tactics or costs?

883. How do you know when you are achieving it?

884. What is your overall strategy for quality control / quality assurance procedures?

885. Is your opponent open to a non-traditional workflow, or will it likely challenge anything you do?

886. What was the rationale for the decision?

887. Linked to original objective?

888. Behaviors; what are guidelines that the team has identified that will assist them with getting the most out of team meetings?

889. How effective is maintaining the log at facilitating organizational learning?

890. How does an increasing emphasis on cost containment influence the strategies and tactics used?

891. Do strategies and tactics aimed at less than full control reduce the costs of management or simply shift the cost burden?

892. What eDiscovery problem or issue did your organization set out to fix or make better?

## 3.5 Quality Audit: Synthetic data

893. How does your organization know that its management of its ethical responsibilities is appropriately effective and constructive?

894. How is the Strategic Plan (and other plans) reviewed and revised?

895. Is there any content that may be legally actionable?

896. How does your organization know that its system for managing intellectual property issues is appropriately effective, constructive and fair?

897. Quality is about improvement and accountability. The immediate questions that arise out of that statement are: (i) improvement on what, and (ii) accountable to whom?

898. Are storage areas and reconditioning operations designed to prevent mix-ups and assure orderly handling of both the distressed and reconditioned devices?

899. How does your organization know that its system for inducting new staff to maximize workplace contributions are appropriately effective and constructive?

900. How does your organization know that its systems for assisting staff with career planning and employment placements are appropriately effective

and constructive?

901. Is progress against the intentions measurable?

902. Is refuse and garbage adequately stored and disposed of with sufficient frequency to prevent contamination?

903. How does your organization know that the system for managing its facilities is appropriately effective and constructive?

904. Are the policies and processes, as set out in the Quality Audit Manual, properly applied?

905. Are the review comments incorporated?

906. How does your organization know that its relationships with relevant professional bodies are appropriately effective and constructive?

907. How does your organization know that its risk management system is appropriately effective and constructive?

908. What happens if your organization fails its Quality Audit?

909. Does the audit organization have experience in performing the required work for entities of your type and size?

910. How does your organization know that its support services planning and management systems are appropriately effective and constructive?

911. How does your organization know that its public relations and marketing systems are appropriately effective and constructive?

912. How does your organization know that its Governance system is appropriately effective and constructive?

## 3.6 Team Directory: Synthetic data

913. Who are your stakeholders (customers, sponsors, end users, team members)?

914. When does information need to be distributed?

915. Who will write the meeting minutes and distribute?

916. How will you accomplish and manage the objectives?

917. Have you decided when to celebrate the Synthetic data projects completion date?

918. Do purchase specifications and configurations match requirements?

919. Timing: when do the effects of communication take place?

920. Who will be the stakeholders on your next Synthetic data project?

921. Process decisions: do invoice amounts match accepted work in place?

922. How does the team resolve conflicts and ensure tasks are completed?

923. Where should the information be distributed?

924. Does a Synthetic data project team directory list

all resources assigned to the Synthetic data project?

925. Process decisions: how well was task order work performed?

926. Contract requirements complied with?

927. Process decisions: which organizational elements and which individuals will be assigned management functions?

928. Process decisions: are there any statutory or regulatory issues relevant to the timely execution of work?

929. Process decisions: are all start-up, turn over and close out requirements of the contract satisfied?

930. Who will report Synthetic data project status to all stakeholders?

# 3.7 Team Operating Agreement: Synthetic data

931. What are some potential sources of conflict among team members?

932. Do you prevent individuals from dominating the meeting?

933. Do you listen for voice tone and word choice to understand the meaning behind words?

934. What types of accommodations will be formulated and put in place for sustaining the team?

935. Are there the right people on your team?

936. Did you draft the meeting agenda?

937. To whom do you deliver your services?

938. Do team members need to frequently communicate as a full group to make timely decisions?

939. Do you send out the agenda and meeting materials in advance?

940. Do you record meetings for the already stated unable to attend?

941. Do you upload presentation materials in advance and test the technology?

942. Do you begin with a question to engage everyone?

943. What are the boundaries (organizational or geographic) within which you operate?

944. Did you recap the meeting purpose, time, and expectations?

945. Did you delegate tasks such as taking meeting minutes, presenting a topic and soliciting input?

946. Confidentiality: how will confidential information be handled?

947. Have you established procedures that team members can follow to work effectively together, such as a team operating agreement?

948. Resource allocation: how will individual team members account for time and expenses, and how will this be allocated in the team budget?

949. What resources can be provided for the team in terms of equipment, space, time for training, protected time and space for meetings, and travel allowances?

950. Do you leverage technology engagement tools group chat, polls, screen sharing, etc.?

## 3.8 Team Performance Assessment: Synthetic data

951. What structural changes have you made or are you preparing to make?

952. To what degree does the team possess adequate membership to achieve its ends?

953. To what degree does the teams approach to its work allow for modification and improvement over time?

954. To what degree can team members frequently and easily communicate with one another?

955. Is there a particular method of data analysis that you would recommend as a means of demonstrating that method variance is not of great concern for a given dataset?

956. Do you give group members authority to make at least some important decisions?

957. To what degree are the goals realistic?

958. To what degree are the members clear on what they are individually responsible for and what they are jointly responsible for?

959. To what degree does the teams work approach provide opportunity for members to engage in fact-based problem solving?

960. When does the medium matter?

961. To what degree does the teams work approach provide opportunity for members to engage in open interaction?

962. What do you think is the most constructive thing that could be done now to resolve considerations and disputes about method variance?

963. What makes opportunities more or less obvious?

964. To what degree will the team adopt a concrete, clearly understood, and agreed-upon approach that will result in achievement of the teams goals?

965. To what degree is there a sense that only the team can succeed?

966. How hard do you try to make a good selection?

967. To what degree will new and supplemental skills be introduced as the need is recognized?

968. To what degree will the team ensure that all members equitably share the work essential to the success of the team?

969. To what degree is the team cognizant of small wins to be celebrated along the way?

970. To what degree will team members, individually and collectively, commit time to help themselves and others learn and develop skills?

## 3.9 Team Member Performance Assessment: Synthetic data

971. How accurately is your plan implemented?

972. What qualities does a successful Team leader possess?

973. To what degree are the goals ambitious?

974. Is there reluctance to join a team?

975. To what degree can team members meet frequently enough to accomplish the teams ends?

976. Who they are?

977. What is collaboration?

978. What kinds of performance factors / elements do you use?

979. Are there any safeguards to prevent intentional or unintentional rating errors?

980. How do you use data to inform instruction and improve staff achievement?

981. How is your organizations Strategic Management System tied to performance measurement?

982. How will they be formed?

983. How are training activities developed from a technical perspective?

984. What is needed for effective data teams?

985. Goals met?

986. Are any validation activities performed?

987. How do you create a self-sustaining capacity for a collaborative culture?

988. What are the evaluation strategies (e.g., reaction, learning, behavior, results) used. What evaluation results did you have?

989. Does adaptive training work?

## 3.10 Issue Log: Synthetic data

990. Do you feel a register helps?

991. Do you feel more overwhelmed by stakeholders?

992. How do you manage communications?

993. Who are the members of the governing body?

994. Are stakeholder roles recognized by your organization?

995. Who is the issue assigned to?

996. In classifying stakeholders, which approach to do so are you using?

997. What is the status of the issue?

998. Which team member will work with each stakeholder?

999. What is the impact on the Business Case?

1000. What would have to change?

1001. What approaches to you feel are the best ones to use?

1002. Who is involved as you identify stakeholders?

1003. What is a change?

1004. How were past initiatives successful?

1005. Why do you manage human resources?

1006. What effort will a change need?

1007. Who were proponents/opponents?

# 4.0 Monitoring and Controlling Process Group: Synthetic data

1008. How is agile portfolio management done?

1009. How are you doing?

1010. What were things that you did very well and want to do the same again on the next Synthetic data project?

1011. Is the program in place as intended?

1012. What are the deliverables?

1013. What are the goals of the program?

1014. Use: how will they use the information?

1015. Did it work?

1016. How can you monitor progress?

1017. How to ensure validity, quality and consistency?

1018. What departments are involved in its daily operation?

1019. What is the timeline for the Synthetic data project?

1020. Are the necessary foundations in place to ensure the sustainability of the results of the programme?

1021. Did you implement the program as designed?

1022. Change, where should you look for problems?

1023. Based on your Synthetic data project communication management plan, what worked well?

1024. Where is the Risk in the Synthetic data project?

# 4.1 Project Performance Report: Synthetic data

1025. To what degree can the cognitive capacity of individuals accommodate the flow of information?

1026. To what degree can team members vigorously define the teams purpose in considerations with others who are not part of the functioning team?

1027. To what degree do team members agree with the goals, relative importance, and the ways in which achievement will be measured?

1028. To what degree does the teams work approach provide opportunity for members to engage in results-based evaluation?

1029. To what degree will each member have the opportunity to advance his or her professional skills in all three of the above categories while contributing to the accomplishment of the teams purpose and goals?

1030. To what degree are sub-teams possible or necessary?

1031. To what degree does the task meet individual needs?

1032. To what degree do individual skills and abilities match task demands?

1033. What is the degree to which rules govern

information exchange between individuals within your organization?

1034. To what degree do members articulate the goals beyond the team membership?

1035. To what degree do the relationships of the informal organization motivate taskrelevant behavior and facilitate task completion?

1036. How will procurement be coordinated with other Synthetic data project aspects, such as scheduling and performance reporting?

1037. What is the PRS?

## 4.2 Variance Analysis: Synthetic data

1038. What is the dollar amount of the fluctuation?

1039. Did a new competitor enter the market?

1040. How are variances affected by multiple material and labor categories?

1041. Does the scheduling system identify in a timely manner the status of work?

1042. Wbs elements contractually specified for reporting of status to your organization (lowest level only)?

1043. Who are responsible for overhead performance control of related costs?

1044. Are there changes in the direct base to which overhead costs are allocated?

1045. What is the budgeted cost for work scheduled?

1046. Are all budgets assigned to control accounts?

1047. How does the monthly budget compare to the actual experience?

1048. Are there knowledgeable Synthetic data projections of future performance?

1049. What are the direct labor dollars and/or hours?

1050. Are your organizations and items of cost assigned to each pool identified?

1051. Does the contractor use objective results, design reviews and tests to trace schedule performance?

## 4.3 Earned Value Status: Synthetic data

1052. If earned value management (EVM) is so good in determining the true status of a Synthetic data project and Synthetic data project its completion, why is it that hardly any one uses it in information systems related Synthetic data projects?

1053. Validation is a process of ensuring that the developed system will actually achieve the stakeholders desired outcomes; Are you building the right product? What do you validate?

1054. What is the unit of forecast value?

1055. Earned value can be used in almost any Synthetic data project situation and in almost any Synthetic data project environment. it may be used on large Synthetic data projects, medium sized Synthetic data projects, tiny Synthetic data projects (in cut-down form), complex and simple Synthetic data projects and in any market sector. some people, of course, know all about earned value, they have used it for years - but perhaps not as effectively as they could have?

1056. How much is it going to cost by the finish?

1057. Where is evidence-based earned value in your organization reported?

1058. When is it going to finish?

1059. Are you hitting your Synthetic data projects targets?

1060. Verification is a process of ensuring that the developed system satisfies the stakeholders agreements and specifications; Are you building the product right? What do you verify?

1061. How does this compare with other Synthetic data projects?

1062. Where are your problem areas?

## 4.4 Risk Audit: Synthetic data

1063. Should additional substantive testing be conducted because of the risk audit results?

1064. How effective are your risk controls?

1065. Which assets are important?

1066. Is there a clear procedure for reporting accidents/injuries?

1067. Do you record and file all audits?

1068. Have all involved been advised of any obligations they have to sponsors?

1069. Is the auditor able to evaluate contradictory evidence in an unbiased manner?

1070. To what extent are auditors effective at linking business risks and management assertions?

1071. Will an appropriate standard of care be applied to all involved?

1072. Is the customer technically sophisticated in the product area?

1073. Are you aware of the industry standards that apply to your operations?

1074. What is happening in other jurisdictions? Could that happen here?

1075. What is the Board doing to assure measurement and improve outcomes and quality and reduce avoidable adverse events?

1076. Has everyone (staff, volunteers and participants) agreed to a code of behaviour or conduct?

1077. For paid staff, does your organization comply with the minimum conditions for employment and/or the applicable modern award?

1078. Have reasonable steps been taken to reduce the risks to acceptable levels?

1079. Is all required equipment available?

1080. The halo effect in business risk audits: can strategic risk assessment bias auditor judgment about accounting details?

1081. Are testing tools available and suitable?

## 4.5 Contractor Status Report: Synthetic data

1082. What are the minimum and optimal bandwidth requirements for the proposed solution?

1083. What is the average response time for answering a support call?

1084. If applicable; describe your standard schedule for new software version releases. Are new software version releases included in the standard maintenance plan?

1085. Who can list a Synthetic data project as organization experience, your organization or a previous employee of your organization?

1086. Are there contractual transfer concerns?

1087. How does the proposed individual meet each requirement?

1088. How is risk transferred?

1089. What was the actual budget or estimated cost for your organizations services?

1090. What process manages the contracts?

1091. What was the overall budget or estimated cost?

1092. What was the final actual cost?

1093. What was the budget or estimated cost for your organizations services?

1094. How long have you been using the services?

1095. Describe how often regular updates are made to the proposed solution. Are corresponding regular updates included in the standard maintenance plan?

## 4.6 Formal Acceptance: Synthetic data

1096. What is the Acceptance Management Process?

1097. Who supplies data?

1098. Was the client satisfied with the Synthetic data project results?

1099. Was the Synthetic data project goal achieved?

1100. Does it do what Synthetic data project team said it would?

1101. General estimate of the costs and times to complete the Synthetic data project?

1102. Was the sponsor/customer satisfied?

1103. Do you buy pre-configured systems or build your own configuration?

1104. Who would use it?

1105. What are the requirements against which to test, Who will execute?

1106. Do you buy-in installation services?

1107. Was business value realized?

1108. What was done right?

1109. Does it do what client said it would?

1110. What features, practices, and processes proved to be strengths or weaknesses?

1111. How does your team plan to obtain formal acceptance on your Synthetic data project?

1112. How well did the team follow the methodology?

1113. Was the Synthetic data project work done on time, within budget, and according to specification?

1114. What can you do better next time?

1115. Did the Synthetic data project manager and team act in a professional and ethical manner?

# 5.0 Closing Process Group: Synthetic data

1116. What areas were overlooked on this Synthetic data project?

1117. How will you know you did it?

1118. How critical is the Synthetic data project success to the success of your organization?

1119. Is this an updated Synthetic data project Proposal Document?

1120. Can the lesson learned be replicated?

1121. How well did the team follow the chosen processes?

1122. What will you do?

1123. How will you do it?

1124. How well did the chosen processes produce the expected results?

1125. What was learned?

1126. Are there funding or time constraints?

1127. Did the Synthetic data project team have the right skills?

1128. Were the outcomes different from the already stated planned?

1129. Does the close educate others to improve performance?

1130. Did the Synthetic data project team have enough people to execute the Synthetic data project plan?

1131. When will the Synthetic data project be done?

1132. Were cost budgets met?

1133. What is the Synthetic data project name and date of completion?

## 5.1 Procurement Audit: Synthetic data

1134. Does the procurement Synthetic data project comply with European Communities regulations and rules?

1135. Does the strategy contain incentives to evaluate the performance of the procurement function/unit?

1136. Was suitability of candidates accurately assessed?

1137. Does the procurement function/unit have the ability to secure best performance from contractors?

1138. When performance conditions were detailed in the tender documentation, did the contracting authority verify if the tenders received met the already stated requirements?

1139. Is your organization policy on purchasing covered by a written manual?

1140. Are outsourcing and Public Private Partnerships considered as alternatives to in-house work?

1141. Is the routing of copies of purchase order forms defined?

1142. Are there any complaints of the suppliers and/or end-users?

1143. Are all mutilated and voided checks retained for proper accounting of pre-numbered checks?

1144. Is the procurement Synthetic data project efficiently managed?

1145. Has your organization examined in detail the definition of performance?

1146. Has an upper limit of cost been fixed?

1147. Are criteria and sub-criteria set suitable to identify the tender that offers best value for money?

1148. Is the accounting distribution of expenses included with the request for payment?

1149. Are order quantities, deliveries and payment levels under the contract monitored by an appropriate official?

1150. Is a cash flow chart prepared and used in determining the timing and term of investments?

1151. Are regulations and protective measures in place to avoid corruption?

1152. Are checks used in numeric sequence?

1153. Was there a sound basis for the scorings applied to the criteria and was the scoring well balanced?

## 5.2 Contract Close-Out: Synthetic data

1154. Change in knowledge?

1155. Has each contract been audited to verify acceptance and delivery?

1156. Parties: Authorized?

1157. Parties: who is involved?

1158. Was the contract sufficiently clear so as not to result in numerous disputes and misunderstandings?

1159. What happens to the recipient of services?

1160. What is capture management?

1161. Are the signers the authorized officials?

1162. Was the contract type appropriate?

1163. How is the contracting office notified of the automatic contract close-out?

1164. Change in circumstances?

1165. Have all contracts been completed?

1166. Have all acceptance criteria been met prior to final payment to contractors?

1167. Change in attitude or behavior?

1168. How does it work?

1169. Was the contract complete without requiring numerous changes and revisions?

1170. Have all contracts been closed?

1171. How/when used ?

1172. Have all contract records been included in the Synthetic data project archives?

1173. Why Outsource?

## 5.3 Project or Phase Close-Out: Synthetic data

1174. What is the information level of detail required for each stakeholder?

1175. Planned remaining costs?

1176. Is the lesson significant, valid, and applicable?

1177. What is in it for you?

1178. Was the schedule met?

1179. What were the goals and objectives of the communications strategy for the Synthetic data project?

1180. What is a Risk Management Process?

1181. What is a Risk?

1182. In preparing the Lessons Learned report, should it reflect a consensus viewpoint, or should the report reflect the different individual viewpoints?

1183. What was the preferred delivery mechanism?

1184. Who controlled the resources for the Synthetic data project?

1185. What information did each stakeholder need to contribute to the Synthetic data projects success?

1186. How much influence did the stakeholder have over others?

1187. What were the desired outcomes?

1188. What hierarchical authority does the stakeholder have in your organization?

1189. Was the user/client satisfied with the end product?

1190. Who exerted influence that has positively affected or negatively impacted the Synthetic data project?

1191. What were the actual outcomes?

1192. What benefits or impacts does the stakeholder group expect to obtain as a result of the Synthetic data project?

## 5.4 Lessons Learned: Synthetic data

1193. Is the lesson based on actual Synthetic data project experience rather than on independent research?

1194. Whom to share Lessons Learned Information with?

1195. How effective was the architecture/system design process?

1196. Was the change control process properly implemented to manage changes to cost, scope, schedule, or quality?

1197. Under what legal authority did your organization head and program manager direct your organization and Synthetic data project?

1198. What was the single greatest success and the single greatest shortcoming or challenge from the Synthetic data projects perspective?

1199. What is the value of the deliverable?

1200. Was the control overhead justified?

1201. How adequately involved did you feel in Synthetic data project decisions?

1202. How useful was the content of the training you received in preparation for the use of the product/ service?

1203. Was the necessary hardware, software, accommodation etc available?

1204. Do you conduct the engineering tests?

1205. How satisfied are you with your involvement in the development and/or review of the Synthetic data project Scope during Synthetic data project Initiation and Planning?

1206. What is in the future?

1207. How well prepared were you to receive Synthetic data project deliverables?

1208. What worked well/did not work well?

1209. What mistakes did you successfully avoid making?

1210. Did the team work well together?

1211. How effective was the documentation that you received with the Synthetic data project product/ service?

# Index

Made in United States
Orlando, FL
04 November 2026

90205875R00166